ILLUSTRATED LIBRARY OF COOKING

VOLUME **3** Bud-Buy

In this book: *well over 100 ways to be creative with ground meats—beef, pork, ham, lamb and veal—ingenious burger and meat loaf recipes, casseroles and skillet dinners . . . PLUS a doubly big budget section that shows how to save money as you shop and cook, how to parlay a pauper's share into surprisingly princely fare.*

ROCKVILLE HOUSE PUBLISHERS, INC.
ROCKVILLE CENTRE, NEW YORK 11570

VOLUME 3

Family Circle®

Illustrated Library of

COOKING

YOUR READY REFERENCE FOR A LIFETIME OF GOOD EATING

Picture Credits:
Ac'cent International • American Frozen Food Institute • General Mills • Pet, Incorporated • Pickle Packers International • Reynolds Wrap

What a beautiful way to use meat balls AND stretch the budget, by teaming them with potatoes, chunks of carrot and zucchini, topping them with a flaky cross-hatch of pastry, then baking in a savory sauce until the flavors mingle.

Table of Contents

BUDGET BOUNTY

BUDGET BOUNTY: PENNY-WISE DINNERS, MEATY MONEY SAVERS, SAVORY MEAT-STRETCHERS, MEAT-STRETCHING SECRETS

It's possible to eat like a prince on a pauper's share. Well, *almost* as the following menus and recipes quickly demonstrate.

Because meat is the biggest single part of the food budget, we concentrate here on money-saving main dishes, most of them surprisingly meaty.

A favorite trick of European gourmet chefs is to take a humble inexpensive cut of meat and turn it into something fit for a king. So many of the dishes we now consider Continental classics were originally simple farmhouse fare—Choucroute Garni . . . Cassoulet . . . Sauerbraten . . . Oxtail Ragout . . . Beef and Kidney Pie.

Budget meats—those from the shank and neck and tail, to name three—have finer flavor, many gourmets insist, than the more lordly rib and loin cuts. And when properly cooked—lazily and long in the company of vegetables and herbs—these budget meats are irresistibly succulent and satisfying.

The bargain meats are unusually versatile, too. They marry well with a long list of vegetables—canned, frozen, fresh and dried. And they partner happily with rice, pasta and such husky grains as barley and cracked wheat, making the food dollar stretch quite magically.

Almost always good buys: pot roasts. Shown here are Twin Pot Roasts, both rolled, one veal and one pork.

HALF A DOZEN PENNY-WISE DINNERS

Twin Pot Roasts
Rich Brown Gravy
Mashed Potatoes
Lima-and-Tomato Scallop
Coleslaw
Upside-Down Peach Ring

Twin Pot Roasts

Flavors of veal and pork blend to complement each other as they braise in one pot.
Makes enough for 2 meals, 6 servings each

- *1 fresh pork shoulder (about 5 pounds), boned and rolled*
- *3½ to 4 pounds rolled, boned, veal shoulder roast*
- *1 tablespoon salt*
- *1 bay leaf*
- *6 whole cloves*
- *4 peppercorns*
- *1 large onion, peeled and quartered*
- *Rich Brown Gravy* (recipe follows)

1 Brown pork slowly in its own fat in heavy kettle or Dutch oven; remove. Brown veal in same kettle. (This will take from 30 to 45 minutes for both meats.)
2 Return pork to kettle, arranging meats side

by side. Season with salt, bay leaf, cloves, peppercorns, and onion. Do not add water; cover.
3 Cook over low heat, turning meats every half hour for even browning, 3½ hours, or until both are tender. Remove to carving board or platter; sprinkle veal with paprika, if you wish. Keep hot while making gravy.

RICH BROWN GRAVY—Pour all fat and juices from kettle into 2-cup measure; let fat rise to top. Skim off fat; return 4 tablespoons fat to kettle. Add water to juices to make 2 cups. Blend 4 tablespoons flour into fat in kettle; cook, stirring all the time, just until mixture bubbles. Stir in the 2 cups liquid slowly; continue cooking and stirring, scraping baked-on juices from bottom and side of kettle, until gravy thickens and boils 1 minute; strain into gravy bowl. Makes 2 cups.

Lima-and-Tomato Scallop

Canned limas and ready-seasoned stewed tomatoes make this quick, economical dish
Bake at 425° for 30 minutes. Makes 6 servings

1 can (about 1 pound) stewed tomatoes
1 can (about 1 pound) green lima beans
2 tablespoons butter or margarine
2 tablespoons flour
½ teaspoon salt
Dash of pepper
1 cup buttered small bread cubes (about 2 slices)

1 Drain liquid from tomatoes and lima beans into a 2-cup measure. (There should be about 1⅓ cups.) Combine vegetables in 6-cup baking dish.
2 Melt butter or margarine over low heat in medium-size saucepan. Stir in flour, salt, and pepper; cook, stirring all the time, just until mixture bubbles. Stir in vegetable liquids; continue cooking and stirring until mixture thickens and boils 1 minute. Pour over vegetables in baking dish; toss lightly with a fork to mix.
3 Bake in hot oven (425°) 15 minutes; sprinkle buttered bread cubes around edge; bake 15 minutes longer, or until bubbly in center.

Upside-Down Peach Ring

Sunny fruit slices circle the top of this fluffy cake to serve warm with tart lemon sauce
Bake at 350° for 40 minutes. Makes 4 to 6 servings

1 can (about 1 pound) cling peach slices
1 cup sifted all-purpose flour
1 teaspoon baking powder
¼ teaspoon salt
¼ cup soft vegetable shortening
½ cup sugar
1 egg
⅛ teaspoon almond extract
⅓ cup milk
Lemon-Butter Topper. (recipe follows)

1 Drain syrup from peaches into a 1-cup measure and set aside for making sauce. Arrange peach slices in a greased 4-cup ring mold.
2 Sift flour, baking powder, and salt onto wax paper.
3 Cream vegetable shortening with sugar until fluffy in a medium-size bowl; beat in egg and almond extract.
4 Stir in dry ingredients, adding alternately with milk, just until blended. Pour over peaches in mold.
5 Bake in moderate oven (350°) 40 minutes, or until top springs back when lightly pressed with fingertip.
6 Cool in mold on a wire rack 15 minutes; cover with serving plate; turn upside down; carefully lift off mold. Cut into wedges; serve warm with *Lemon-Butter Topper*.

LEMON-BUTTER TOPPER—Combine 2 tablespoons bottled lemon juice with saved peach syrup; add water, if needed, to make 1 cup. Blend a few spoonfuls into 1 tablespoon cornstarch in a small saucepan, then stir in remaining. Cook, stirring constantly, until sauce thickens and boils 3 minutes; stir in 1 tablespoon butter or margarine. Makes about 1 cup.

Gourmet Chicken Breasts with
Mushroom Gravy
Turn-About Macaroni Loaf
Peas Parisienne
Lettuce Wedges
Russian Dressing
Baked Plum Whip with
Sun-Gold Sauce

Gourmet Chicken Breasts

A glamour dish if there ever was one!
Bake at 350° for 1 hour. Makes 6 servings

3 whole broiler-fryers, about 2 pounds each
Gourmet Stuffing (recipe follows)
4 tablespoons (½ stick) butter or margarine
½ cup packaged cornflake crumbs
1 can or 1 envelope (2 to a package) mushroom-soup mix

1 Cut up each chicken this way: With sharp knife or kitchen scissors, cut off legs at thigh joints, then separate drumsticks and thighs. Next, cut through second joints of wings and remove pieces with wing tips, leaving the small "drumsticks" attached to breast. Holding chicken, breast side up, cut through thin sides and ribs to separate back from breast. Break back in half, then set aside with legs, thighs, wing tips, gizzard, and neck for *Country Fricassee.* Save liver for stuffing.

2 Halve breast this way: Pull off skin, then cut along breastbone on either side, loosening meat as you go, until each side can be pulled away in one piece. Snip out small bones. Pull each half breast open in middle to form a pocket for stuffing. (Meat will come apart easily between its 2 large muscles.)

3 Make *Gourmet Stuffing* . Spoon into breast pockets to fill; press edges together and fasten with wooden picks.

4 Melt butter or margarine in large shallow baking pan; roll chicken in butter to coat well; arrange in single layer in same pan. Sprinkle crumbs over top.

5 Bake in moderate oven (350°) 1 hour, or until chicken is tender and golden.

6 Prepare mushroom-soup mix, following label directions for gravy or sauce.

7 Place chicken on heated serving platter; remove wooden picks. Pass gravy in separate bowl to spoon over chicken.

Gourmet Stuffing
Makes 2 cups

3 chicken livers
4 tablespoons (½ stick) butter or margarine
2 cups soft bread crumbs (4 slices)
2 tablespoons chopped onion
1 tablespoon water
1 teaspoon Worcestershire sauce
½ teaspoon salt

1 Sauté chicken livers in butter or margarine, stirring often, in small frying pan 5 minutes, or until livers lose their pink color.

2 Remove livers and chop, then add to bread crumbs in medium-size bowl. Sauté onion just until soft in same frying pan.

3 Stir water, Worcestershire sauce, and salt into onions in frying pan; pour over crumb mixture. Toss lightly to mix well. (Mixture will be crumbly, not wet.)

Turn-About Macaroni Loaf
Recipe gives a speedy trick for turning macaroni into a handsome mold
Makes 6 servings

Budget-stretching chicken given a gourmet treatment.

1 package (8 ounces) elbow macaroni
¼ cup grated process cheese spread (from an 8-ounce package)
2 tablespoons mayonnaise or salad dressing
½ teaspoon prepared mustard
½ teaspoon salt
⅛ teaspoon pepper
½ cup chopped parsley

1 Cook macaroni in large amount boiling salted water, following label directions; drain; return to kettle.
2 Stir in cheese spread, mayonnaise or salad dressing, mustard, salt, and pepper, tossing until well-mixed and cheese is melted. Sprinkle parsley over; stir in lightly.
3 Spoon into a shallow 4-cup mold or loaf pan, 9x5x3, pressing down firmly; let stand in warm place about 5 minutes. Cover mold with serving plate; turn upside down; lift off mold.

Peas Parisienne
For the best-ever summer-fresh flavor, cook this favorite vegetable in the oven
Bake at 350° for 1 hour. Makes 6 servings

2 packages (10 ounces each) frozen green peas
1 teaspoon salt
1 teaspoon sugar
2 tablespoons butter or margarine
1 large lettuce leaf
1 bunch of radishes, trimmed and sliced thin (about 1 cup)

1 Place peas in 6-cup baking dish; sprinkle with salt and sugar. Dot with butter or margarine; top with lettuce leaf.
2 Bake, covered, in moderate oven (350°) 1 hour, or until tender.
3 Remove lettuce; stir in radish slices.

Always a penny-saver: pasta. Shown here is a browned and bubbling Manicotti.

Baked Plum Whip
It's light, fruity, and just a bit tart. A special ingredient short-cuts fixing
Bake at 350° for 40 minutes. Makes 6 servings

2 egg whites
Dash of salt
⅓ cup sugar
1 jar (about 4 ounces) baby-pack strained plums
1 tablespoon lemon juice
Red food coloring
Sun-Gold Sauce (recipe follows)

1 Beat egg whites and salt until foamy-white and double in volume in medium-size bowl. Sprinkle in sugar *very slowly,* 1 tablespoon at a time, beating all the time until sugar completely dissolves and meringue stands in firm peaks. (Save yolks for making sauce.)
2 Fold in plums and lemon juice, then a few drops red food coloring to tint mixture a delicate pink. Pour into buttered 6-cup baking dish.
3 Place dish in baking pan on oven shelf; pour boiling water into pan to depth of about an inch.
4 Bake in moderate oven (350°) 40 minutes, or just until firm in center.
5 Unmold onto serving plate. Serve warm with *Sun-Gold Sauce.*

SUN-GOLD SAUCE—Beat 2 egg yolks with ¼ cup sugar until fluffy in top of double boiler. Stir in ½ cup orange juice and 2 tablespoons lemon juice. Cook, stirring constantly, over simmering, *not boiling,* water until mixture thickens slightly and coats a metal spoon. Remove from heat; strain into small bowl; cool to lukewarm. Whip ½ cup cream until stiff in small bowl; fold into custard. Serve warm. Makes about 2 cups.

Simple but Festive
Manicotti
Onion-Ring Salad Bowl
Crusty Bread Chunks
Frosty Orange Sherbet

Manicotti
Meat-seasoned sauce from stuffed beef roll is ready. Recipe has a speedy trick for filling the big tubular noodles
Bake at 350° for 40 minutes. Makes 8 servings

1 package (12 ounces) manicotti noodles
2 cups (1 pound) cream-style cottage cheese
1 package (8 ounces) cream cheese
1 package (9 ounces) frozen chopped spinach, thawed and drained
¼ pound liverwurst, diced
2 eggs
1 teaspoon salt
⅛ teaspoon pepper
6 cups tomato sauce (from Stuffed Beef Roll; recipe follows)
1 package (8 ounces) sliced mozzarella or pizza cheese, cut into triangles

1 Cook manicotti noodles, a few at a time, in large amount of boiling salted water, following label directions; lift out carefully with slotted spoon so as not to break; place in pan of cold water until ready to fill.
2 Mix cottage cheese, cream cheese, spinach, liverwurst, eggs, salt, and pepper until well-blended in medium-size bowl. Heat tomato sauce in medium-size saucepan; keep hot for Step 4.
3 Lift manicotti noodles, 1 at a time, from water; drain. Fill with cheese mixture, using a long-handle teaspoon. (Or fill a plastic bag with cheese mixture; fold to make a cone-shape and snip an opening in one corner. Squeeze filling into noodles.)
4 Arrange filled noodles in rows in a single layer in 16-cup shallow baking pan. Spoon hot tomato sauce over and around noodles; cover.
5 Bake in moderate oven (350°) 30 minutes; uncover; arrange cheese triangles, overlapping, on noodles.
6 Bake 10 minutes longer, or until cheese is melted and bubbly-hot.

NOTE: To make ahead, cook and stuff noodles. Place in baking pan; spoon tomato sauce over; cover; chill. Remove from refrigerator and let stand at room temperature 30 minutes. Bake, covered, in moderate oven (350°) 50 minutes; uncover. Place cheese on top; bake 10 minutes longer, or until bubbly-hot.

Onion-Ring Salad Bowl
Simply toss crisp greens and nippy onions with zesty dressing to make this favorite
Makes 8 servings

1 medium-size head of iceberg lettuce
1 medium-size head of romaine
4 small white onions, peeled, sliced thin, and separated into rings
1 envelope Italian salad-dressing mix
Vegetable oil
Cider vinegar

1 Break lettuce and romaine leaves into bite-size pieces in large salad bowl. Top with onion rings.

2 Prepare Italian salad-dressing mix with vegetable oil, vinegar, and water, following label directions. Pour ⅓ cup over salad; toss to mix well. Serve at once. (Store remaining dressing in covered jar in refrigerator for another salad.)

Crusty Bread Chunks
Fresh-from-the-oven hot bread is a breeze to "bake" this way
Bake at 350° for 15 minutes. Makes 8 servings

1 loaf Italian bread
3 tablespoons vegetable oil
½ teaspoon seasoned salt

1 Cut loaf of Italian bread in half lengthwise, then quarter each half crosswise. Set pieces, bottom crust down, on cutting board; cut in ½-inch-thick slices almost through.
2 Combine vegetable oil and seasoned salt in a cup; brush lightly over all cut surfaces of bread. Re-form into loaf shape; wrap in foil.
3 Bake in moderate oven (350°) 15 minutes, or until hot.

Frosty Orange Sherbet
It tastes so cool, tangy, and refreshing after an Italian-style dinner
Makes 8 servings

1½ cups milk
½ cup sugar
¼ cup light corn syrup
¼ teaspoon salt
6 tablespoons frozen concentrated orange juice (from a 6-ounce can)
¼ cup lemon juice
2 egg whites

1 Heat milk, sugar, corn syrup, and salt, stirring constantly, in medium-size saucepan, just until sugar dissolves. Remove from heat.
2 Stir in frozen concentrated orange juice and lemon juice. (Mixture will look curdled, but flecks will disappear when frozen.)
3 Pour into 2 ice-cube trays or pan, 8x8x2; freeze, stirring several times, about 2 hours, or until almost firm.
4 Beat egg whites until they stand in firm peaks in small bowl.
5 Spoon sherbet into a chilled large bowl; beat until fluffy; fold in egg whites.
6 Return to trays; freeze 2 to 3 hours longer, or until firm.

Stuffed Beef Roll
Baked Potatoes
Golden Turnip Scallop
Chopped Lettuce Salad
Chocolate-Pudding Puff

Stuffed Beef Roll
With its herb stuffing, each slice looks like a giant pinwheel. Meat choice is thrifty flank steak
Makes 6 servings

1 flank steak (1½ to 2 pounds)
3 medium-size onions, chopped (1½ cups)
4 tablespoons (½ stick) butter or margarine
2 cups ready-mix bread stuffing (half an 8-ounce package)
¼ cup chopped parsley
2 tablespoons grated Parmesan cheese
½ teaspoon garlic salt
½ cup water
¼ cup unsifted all-purpose flour
¼ cup vegetable oil
2 envelopes spaghetti-sauce mix
4 cups tomato juice (from a 46-ounce can)
1 can (about 2 pounds) Italian tomatoes
2 cans (3 or 4 ounces each) mushroom stems and pieces

1 Ask your meatman to split flank steak, butterfly fashion. Or you can do it yourself with a sharp long-blade knife. Work slowly, cutting with a sawing motion, as evenly as possible.
2 Sauté ¼ cup onion in butter or margarine just until soft in medium-size saucepan. (Save remaining onion for sauce in Step 5.) Stir in bread stuffing, parsley, Parmesan cheese, garlic salt, and water; toss with fork until moist and well-mixed.
3 Lay steak flat on counter top; spread stuffing over steak to within 1 inch of edges. Starting at one end, roll up, jelly-roll style; fasten with 2 or 3 wooden picks. Fold up ends of roll to hold in stuffing; fasten with more wooden picks.
4 Rub roll well with flour; brown in vegetable oil in heavy kettle or Dutch oven.
5 Stir in saved 1¼ cups onion; sauté just until soft. Stir in spaghetti-sauce mix, tomato juice, tomatoes, and mushrooms and liquid; cover. Simmer 1½ hours, or until meat is tender.
6 Remove roll to carving board; take out wooden picks. Carve meat in ½-inch-thick slices. Measure out and chill 6 cups sauce for *Manicotti (recipe precedes).* Serve remaining with meat roll.

Beef isn't budget fare unless *it's a not-so-tender cut like flank steak cleverly extended with a cheesey-herby stuffing, rolled up, tied and pot roasted in a Dutch oven with a zippy mushroom and tomato sauce.*

Golden Turnip Scallop
Peppery turnip, mellowed with apple, bakes buttery-sweet in this easy vegetable dish
Bake at 350° for 1½ hours. Makes 6 servings

6 cups shredded raw yellow turnip (about 1½ pounds)
1 apple, pared, quartered, cored, and chopped
2 tablespoons brown sugar
1 teaspoon salt
⅛ teaspoon pepper
4 tablespoons (½ stick) butter or margarine

1 Mix turnip, ¾ of the chopped apple, brown sugar, salt, and pepper in 6-cup baking dish.
2 Sprinkle remaining chopped apple in a ring on top; dot with butter or margarine; cover.
3 Bake in moderate oven (350°) 1½ hours, or until turnip is tender.

Chocolate-Pudding Puff
Rich, moist, and delicately light, it tastes just like a chocolate soufflé
Bake at 350° for 1 hour and 10 minutes. Makes 6 servings

½ cup sugar
3 tablespoons flour
½ teaspoon salt

Memories are made of this—an old-fashioned chicken fricassee, made of cost-cutting wings, thighs and backs.

- *2 cups milk*
- *2 tablespoons butter or margarine*
- *2 squares unsweetened chocolate*
- *2 eggs, separated*
- *2 cups soft bread crumbs (about 4 slices with crusts removed)*
- *1 teaspoon vanilla*

1 Combine sugar, flour, and salt in medium-size saucepan; stir in a little milk until mixture is well-blended and smooth, then stir in remaining. Add butter or margarine and chocolate.
2 Cook, stirring constantly, over medium heat until chocolate melts and mixture bubbles; remove from heat.
3 Beat egg yolks with fork in small bowl; stir in a generous ½ cup of hot mixture; quickly stir back into mixture in saucepan. Cook, stirring constantly, 1 minute longer, or until slightly thick.
4 Stir in bread crumbs and vanilla; pour into medium-size bowl; let stand 10 minutes to cool slightly.
5 Beat egg whites until they stand in firm peaks in medium-size bowl; fold into cooled chocolate mixture until no streaks of white remain. Pour into greased 6-cup baking dish.
6 Set baking dish in a baking pan; place on oven shelf; pour boiling water into pan to depth of about an inch.
7 Bake in moderate oven (350°) 1 hour and 10 minutes, or until a knife inserted in center comes out clean. Serve warm, plain or with cream or ice cream.

Country Fricassee
Fluffy Paprika Dumplings
Buttered Carrot Sticks
Apple-Celery Salad
Lemon Fluff Tarts

Country Fricassee

Tender chicken, dumpling puffs, and savory rich gravy all cook in the same kettle
Makes 6 servings

Drumsticks, thighs, wing tips, and back pieces from 3 broiler-fryers (about 2 pounds each)
1 large onion, peeled and sliced
1 cup diced celery and leaves
1 tablespoon salt
⅛ teaspoon pepper
2 cups water (for chicken)
½ cup water (for gravy)
¼ cup sifted all-purpose flour
Fluffy Paprika Dumplings (recipe follows)
Paprika

1 Place chicken pieces, onion, celery and leaves, salt, pepper, and 2 cups water in kettle or Dutch oven; cover. Heat to boiling, then simmer 1 hour, or until chicken is tender.
2 Remove chicken from broth; cool until easy to handle; slip off skin from large pieces, if you wish. Pick meat from bony pieces and discard bones. Save meat for Step 5.
3 Strain broth into a 4-cup measure; add water, if needed, to make 4 cups. Press vegetables through strainer into broth; return to kettle; heat to boiling.
4 Stir ½ cup cold water into flour in cup to make a smooth paste; stir into hot broth. Cook, stirring constantly, until gravy thickens and boils 1 minute.
5 Return chicken to kettle; heat slowly to boiling while stirring up *Fluffy Paprika Dumplings*.
6 Drop batter into 6 mounds on top of chicken. Cook, covered, 20 minutes. (No peeking, or they won't steam puffy-light.)
7 Sprinkle dumplings with paprika; garnish with parsley, if you like; serve from kettle. Or arrange chicken and dumplings on a heated serving platter, then garnish. Pass gravy separately.

FLUFFY PAPRIKA DUMPLINGS—Sift 2 cups sifted all-purpose flour, 3 teaspoons baking powder, 1 teaspoon salt, and ¼ teaspoon paprika into medium-size bowl; cut in 2 tablespoons vegetable shortening with pastry blender until mixture is crumbly. Stir in 1 cup milk just until mixture is moist. (Dough will be soft.)

Apple-Celery Salad

This favorite looks extra inviting when served in bowls lined with apple slices
Makes 6 servings

3 medium-size tart apples
1½ cups sliced celery
½ cup chopped walnuts
¼ cup mayonnaise or salad dressing
2 teaspoons sugar
Dash of ground allspice
1 teaspoon lemon juice

1 Pare, quarter, core, and dice 2 apples. (Save remaining apple for Step 3.) Place in medium-size bowl; stir in celery and walnuts.
2 Blend remaining ingredients in 1-cup measure; pour over apple mixture; toss lightly to mix.
3 Quarter and core saved apple; cut into thin slices.
4 Fill individual salad bowls with apple mixture, dividing evenly; garnish with a stand-up ring of apple slices around edges. Top each with a halved walnut, if you wish.

A classic cents-saving combo: apples and celery in a salad.

Lemon Fluff Tarts

Each little shell holds a tart chiffonlike filling.
Your starter—pie-filling mix
Bake at 425° for 15 minutes. Makes 6 tarts

1 package piecrust mix
1 package lemon-flavor pudding and pie-filling mix
Sugar (for filling)
Water
2 eggs, separated
2 tablespoons butter or margarine
1 teaspoon vanilla
¼ cup sugar (for meringue)

1 Prepare piecrust mix, following label directions, or make pastry from your own favorite one-crust recipe.
2 Roll out, half at a time, to ¼-inch thickness on lightly floured pastry cloth or board; cut each into 3 six-inch rounds, using a saucer for pattern. Fit into 4-inch tart-shell pans, pressing firmly against bottoms and sides; trim any overhang. Prick well all over with a fork.
3 Bake in hot oven (425°) 15 minutes, or until golden; cool in pans on wire rack, then remove carefully.
4 Combine pie-filling mix and sugar in medium-size saucepan, following label directions for pie filling; stir in ½ cup less liquid than called for on package; beat in egg yolks. (Save egg whites for Step 5.) Cook, following label directions; remove from heat. Stir in butter or margarine and vanilla; cool.
5 Beat egg whites until foamy-white and double in volume in medium-size bowl; sprinkle in sugar *very slowly,* 1 tablespoon at a time, beating all the time until sugar completely dissolves and

To give leftovers an un-leftover look, take any leftover meat roast—beef, veal, lamb, pork or ham and "reroast" à la Sweet-and-Spicy Meats (recipe at left), basting often with a glisteny sweet-sour sauce made with soy and vinegar.

meringue forms soft peaks. Fold into cooled pudding mixture until no streaks of white appear.
6 Spoon into cooled tart shells, making deep swirls on tops with tip of spoon; chill 1 hour, or until set.

●

Sweet-and-Spicy Meats
Spoon Bread Cups
Squash Moons with Crab Apples
Spinach-Tomato Salad Mimosa
Orange-Rice Cream

Sweet-and-Spicy Meats

Leftovers were never better! Slice meat, then glaze with a soy-rich sauce
Bake at 400° about 30 minutes. Makes 6 servings

2 tablespoons vegetable oil
2 tablespoons soy sauce
2 tablespoons molasses
1 tablespoon cider vinegar
1 small onion, chopped (¼ cup)
12 slices cooked pork, veal, lamb, ham or beef or a combination

1 Combine vegetable oil, soy sauce, molasses, vinegar, and onion in small saucepan. Heat to boiling, then simmer, uncovered, 8 to 10 minutes, or until reduced by about half.
2 Arrange meat slices, slightly overlapping, in large shallow baking pan; brush with about ⅓ of sauce mixture.
3 Bake in hot oven (400°), brushing 2 or 3 times with remaining sauce and pan drippings, 30 minutes, or until heated through and lightly glazed.

●

Spoon Bread Cups

Bake at 400° for 25 minutes. Makes 6 servings

¾ cup yellow cornmeal
1½ cups boiling water
2 tablespoons butter or margarine
¾ cup milk
3 eggs, slightly beaten
2 teaspoons baking powder
1 teaspoon salt

1 Place cornmeal in large bowl; pour boiling water over, stirring until thick and smooth.
2 Stir in butter or margarine, milk, eggs, baking powder, and salt; beat until well blended. Pour into 6 buttered 6-ounce custard or soufflé cups; set, not touching, on a cooky sheet for easy handling.
3 Bake in hot oven (400°) 25 minutes, or until almost set but still soft in center. Serve hot.

Squash Moons With Crab Apples

Acorn squash and rosy crab apples are thrifty plattermates.
Bake at 400° for 40 minutes. Makes 6 servings

2 medium-size acorn squashes
4 tablespoons (½ stick) butter or margarine
1 teaspoon salt
6 spiced crab apples (from a 1-pound jar)

1 Cut each squash crosswise into 6 even slices with large heavy-blade knife; scoop out seeds and stringy membrane, but do not pare.
2 Melt butter or margarine in large shallow baking pan. Arrange squash slices in single layer in pan, turning to coat both sides; sprinkle with salt. Cover pan with lid or foil, fastening around edges of pan to seal tightly.
3 Bake in hot oven (400°) 30 minutes, or until tender. Uncover; add crab apples; brush squash and apples with drippings in pan. Bake 10 minutes longer, or until crab apples are heated through.

●

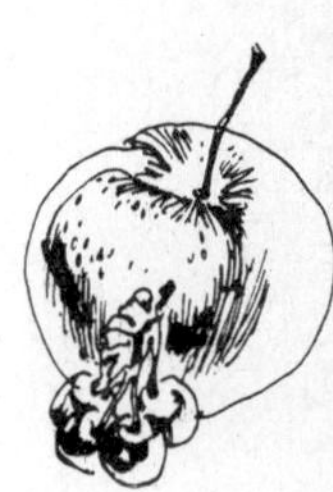

Spinach-Tomato Salad Mimosa

Pretty, nutritious, and inexpensive!
Makes 6 servings

1 package (10 ounces) fresh spinach
1 can (about 1 pound) whole tomatoes
1 hard-cooked egg, shelled
1 tablespoon sugar
1 teaspoon salt
¼ teaspoon pepper
2 tablespoons cider vinegar
1 tablespoon water

1 Remove coarse stems from spinach; break leaves into bite-size pieces in salad bowl.
2 Empty tomatoes into a shallow dish; set the largest, most perfect one aside for garnish. Chop remaining coarsely; add to spinach. (Use juice from can for beverage.)
3 Dice white of egg and add to spinach. Sieve yolk; pile into top of saved whole tomato.
4 Mix sugar, salt, pepper, vinegar, and water in a cup; pour over salad; toss to mix well. Garnish with egg-topped whole tomato.

●

Orange-Rice Cream

Fresh fruit gives this dessert an extra-special flavor zip
Makes 6 servings

½ cup uncooked regular rice
1 teaspoon salt
1½ cups water
½ medium-size seedless orange
2 eggs

½ cup sugar
½ cup seedless raisins
2 cups milk
1 teaspoon vanilla
Nutmeg

1 Combine rice, salt, and water in top of double boiler; heat to boiling over direct heat, then cook 30 minutes, or until tender.
2 Squeeze juice from orange half into cup. Cut up peel, then chop enough very fine to measure 2 tablespoons; stir into orange juice.
3 Beat eggs slightly in medium-size bowl; stir in sugar, raisins, milk, and vanilla until well-blended.
4 Stir egg mixture and orange juice and peel into rice in top of double boiler; place over simmering water.
5 Cook, stirring constantly, 15 minutes, or until mixture thickens and coats a metal spoon.
6 Spoon into 6 serving dishes; sprinkle with nutmeg. Serve warm or chilled.

SOME MEATY MONEY-SAVERS

Choucroute Garni
Makes 6 servings

2 cans (1 pound, 11 ounces each) sauerkraut
6 ham hocks, weighing about 3 pounds
2 cups dry white wine
1 bay leaf
6 whole cloves
1 medium-size onion, peeled
1½ pounds knockwurst
1 red apple, quartered, cored, and sliced
12 new potatoes (about 1¼ pounds)

1 Soak sauerkraut 5 minutes in cold water in a large bowl; drain well.
2 Place ham hocks in a Dutch oven or a large heat-proof casserole. Add drained sauerkraut, wine and bay leaf. Press cloves into onion; press onion down into sauerkraut. Heat to boiling; reduce heat; cover. Simmer very slowly 1½ hours, tossing with a fork once or twice, or until ham hocks are almost tender.
3 Score knockwurst with a sharp knife; place

Choucroute Garni is a robust Alsatian dish that has, within the last few years, ascended to gourmetdom.

on sauerkraut; simmer 20 minutes longer. Add apple slices, pushing them down into sauerkraut; cook 10 minutes longer.
4 Scrub potatoes well; cook in boiling salted water to cover in a medium-size saucepan 20 minutes, or until done.
5 Arrange choucroute with potatoes on a large deep platter. Serve with whole-wheat bread and mustard, if you wish.

Easy Sauerbraten

When chuck roast is on special, buy a bone-in roast about 2 inches thick and weighing about 5 pounds, and divide it for two meals. Cut along the blade bone. Use the larger portion for Easy Sauerbraten, and the smaller, more tender, portion for *Beef Stroganoff With Dill (recipe follows)*
Makes 6 servings

3½ pounds chuck roast
1 cup cider vinegar
¾ cup red wine
2 teaspoons salt
¼ teaspoon seasoned pepper
6 whole allspice
1 large onion, chopped (1 cup)
1 cup chopped carrots (2 medium)
½ cup chopped celery
3 tablespoons flour
2 tablespoons vegetable oil
8 gingersnaps, crushed (⅔ cup)

1 Tie meat securely around edge with string to keep its shape. Place in a large glass or pottery bowl.
2 Mix vinegar, wine, salt, pepper and allspice in a 4-cup measure; pour over meat; add vegetables; cover. Chill 24 hours, turning meat several times.
3 When ready to cook meat, remove from marinade (if muscles in meat seem to separate, push long metal skewers through meat); sprinkle both sides of meat with flour; pat with hands to make an even coating. Brown on both sides in hot oil in deep skillet or Dutch oven. Pour marinade with vegetables over; heat to boiling; reduce heat; cover.
4 Simmer 2½ to 3 hours, or until meat is very tender. Remove meat to heated serving platter; keep warm.
5 Strain liquid into a 4-cup measure; let stand a few minutes until fat rises to top, skim off fat; return liquid to pan. Press vegetables through a sieve and stir in with crushed gingersnaps. Heat, stirring constantly, until gravy thickens and is bubbly-hot.
6 Remove strings and skewers from meat. Carve meat into ¼-inch-thick slices. Serve gravy separately to spoon over.

Beef Stroganoff With Dill

Tender little strips of meat, still rare inside, combine with a creamy sauce fragrant with dill.
Makes 6 servings

1½ pounds chuck roast
4 tablespoons (½ stick) butter or margarine
1 large onion, chopped (1 cup)
¼ pound mushrooms, sliced
3 tablespoons flour
2 cups water
2 envelopes or teaspoons instant beef broth
½ teaspoon salt
⅛ teaspoon pepper
1 cup (8-ounce carton) dairy sour cream
2 tablespoons chopped fresh dill
OR: 1 teaspoon dillweed

1 Cut meat into 2x¼-inch strips. Heat butter or margarine in a large skillet; add meat, one third at a time, and sauté quickly, 2 to 3 minutes, or until brown but still rare inside; remove with a slotted spoon and keep warm.
2 Add onion and mushrooms to skillet and sauté until golden, about 6 to 8 minutes. Stir in flour; gradually stir in water.
3 Heat, stirring constantly, until sauce thickens and bubbles 3 minutes; stir in instant beef broth, salt, pepper and sour cream. Heat slowly, just until piping hot; do not boil.
4 Add beef and dill or dillweed. Serve with cooked rice or noodles and garnish with dill, if you wish.

Braised Stuffed Breast Of Veal

A wonderful way to prepare this low-cost meat—delightfully stuffed, braised and sauced.
Makes 8 servings

1 boned breast of veal (about 2¼ pounds)
¾ teaspoon salt
⅛ teaspoon pepper
2 tablespoons chopped parsley
½ teaspoon leaf basil, crumbled
½ pound sausage meat (from a 1 pound package)
1 cup grated carrots (about 3 large carrots)
1 tablespoon butter or margarine
½ cup sliced celery
1 medium-size onion, sliced

1 can (about 14 ounces) chicken broth
Water
3 tablespoons flour

1 Spread breast of veal flat on a cutting board. (It should measure about 8 inches by 15 inches.) Sprinkle with salt, pepper, parsley and basil. Combine sausage meat with grated carrots in a small bowl; spread evenly over surface of veal, pressing firmly. Roll up veal from short end, jelly-roll fashion. Tie crosswise with heavy string at 1½-inch intervals.
2 Brown meat in butter or margarine in Dutch oven; add celery and onion; sauté 5 minutes longer. Add chicken broth; simmer, covered, 2 hours, or until meat is tender. Remove meat to a carving board.
3 Strain pan juices through a sieve; press vegetables through; pour into a 2-cup measure; add water if necessary to make 1¾ cups. Return to Dutch oven.
4 Combine flour and 6 tablespoons water in a 1-cup measure; blend until smooth. Pour into juices in Dutch oven. Cook, stirring constantly, until sauce thickens and bubbles 3 minutes.
5 Remove string from veal; cut into thin slices; serve with vegetable sauce.

●

Deviled Veal Ribs

Pick up these crispies in your fingers and nibble them right down to the bone. They're that good! Bake at 325° for 2 hours, then at 400° for 20 minutes. Makes 4 servings

Two bountiful dishes for budget watchers: Deviled Veal Ribs, crispy-brown underneath a crumb coating, and Country Lamb Dinner, meaty lamb shanks braised with vegetables.

4 pounds breast of veal
Seasoned salt
Seasoned pepper
6 slices bread
¼ cup lemon juice
¼ cup prepared mustard
¼ cup vegetable oil

1 Cut breast of veal between each rib into strips; sprinkle lightly with seasoned salt and pepper. Place in a single layer in a large shallow baking pan.
2 Bake in slow oven (325°) 2 hours, or until meat is tender. Remove from oven; raise temperature to hot (400°).
3 While meat bakes, toast bread slices on a cooky sheet in same oven 15 minutes, or until hard and dry. Cool; roll into fine crumbs. (Tip for easy cleanup: Break bread into chunks and place in a plastic bag; seal; crush with a rolling pin.)
4 Blend lemon juice, mustard, and vegetable oil in a cup; brush part over ribs to coat both sides; sprinkle with half of the bread crumbs.
5 Bake in hot oven (400°) 10 minutes, or until golden; turn. Brush with remaining mustard mixture and sprinkle with remaining crumbs. Bake 10 minutes longer, or until crispy-brown. Pile into a napkin-lined basket or onto a heated serving platter.

Country Lamb Dinner
Meaty shanks, five vegetables, and zippy gravy make this inviting platter meal
Makes 4 servings

4 lamb shanks, weighing about 3 pounds
1 clove garlic, minced
4 cups water
2 teaspoons salt
1 teaspoon of oregano, crumbled
4 medium-size potatoes, pared
8 small onions, peeled
6 medium-size carrots, pared and quartered lengthwise
1 small head cabbage
1 can (1 pound) sliced beets
Horseradish Gravy (recipe follows)

1 Brown lamb shanks in a kettle or Dutch oven; push to one side. Stir garlic into drippings and sauté until soft.
2 Stir in water, salt, and oregano; cover. Simmer 1 hour, or until meat is almost tender.
3 Lay potatoes and onions around meat in kettle; cover. Cook 30 minutes; add carrots; cook 15 minutes.
4 Quarter cabbage; cut out core; place wedges in kettle; cover. Cook 15 minutes longer, or until meat and all vegetables are tender.
5 Heat beets in a small saucepan; drain.
6 Lift lamb shanks and vegetables from kettle with a slotted spoon and arrange with beets on a heated large serving platter; sprinkle potatoes with paprika, if you wish. Keep hot while making gravy.

HORSERADISH GRAVY—Strain broth from kettle into a 2-cup measure; add water, if needed, to make 1½ cups. Melt 2 tablespoons butter or margarine in a small saucepan; stir in 2 tablespoons flour, 1 teaspoon dillweed, and ½ teaspoon salt; cook, stirring constantly, just until bubbly. Stir in the 1½ cups broth; continue cooking and stirring until gravy thickens and boils 1 minute. Stir in 1 tablespoon prepared horseradish and a few drops bottled gravy coloring to darken, if you wish. Makes about 1¾ cups.

Lamb Shanks Provencale
Inexpensive lamb shanks and mealy beans combine in a bubbly dinner casserole.
Bake at 350° for 2 hours. Makes 6 servings

1 package (1 pound) dried lima beans or Great Northern white beans
8 cups water
3 medium-size onions, chopped (1½ cups)
2 tablespoons vegetable oil
1 can (1 pound) tomatoes
3 teaspoons salt
1 teaspoon leaf savory, crumbled
2 cloves of garlic, slivered
6 lamb shanks (3½ to 4 pounds)
½ cup water

1 Combine beans with water in a kettle; heat to boiling; boil 2 minutes; cover. Remove from heat; let stand 1 hour.
2 Heat beans to boiling again; reduce heat; cover. Simmer 1½ hours, or until tender. Drain, reserving liquid. Place beans in a large shallow baking dish.
3 Sauté onion in oil until golden, about 8 minutes, in a large skillet. Add to beans; stir in tomatoes, salt and savory.
4 Insert garlic slivers in lamb shanks. Brown shanks on all sides, in same skillet; arrange on top of beans. Pour off all fat from skillet; add water; heat, stirring constantly to loosen browned bits; add to beans. Add enough of reserved liquid to come just to top of beans.
5 Bake, uncovered, in moderate oven (350°) 2 hours, or until meat is tender, stirring occasionally with fork. Add more liquid if needed. Garnish with parsley, if you wish.

Curried Pork Kebabs
Season meat cubes in a soy-sparked sauce, broil juicy-tender, and serve atop delicate barley pilaf
Makes 6 servings

1 piece fresh pork shoulder, weighing about 3 pounds
2 teaspoons curry powder
1 tablespoon vegetable oil
⅓ cup soy sauce
⅓ cup water
2 tablespoons cider vinegar
Unseasoned instant meat tenderizer
Barley Pilaf (recipe follows)
Spiced whole crab apples

1 Trim fat and remove bone from pork shoulder; cut meat into 1½-inch cubes. Place in a large shallow dish.
2 Cook curry powder in vegetable oil in a small saucepan 1 minute; stir in soy sauce, water, and vinegar; heat to boiling. Pour over pork cubes; turn cubes to coat completely. Chill at least 4 hours to season.
3 When ready to cook pork, remove from marinade and place on wax paper; set marinade aside for next step. Sprinkle meat with tenderizer, following label directions. Thread onto 6 long skewers, dividing evenly. Place on rack in broiler pan.
4 Broil, 6 inches from heat, turning and brushing often with marinade from dish, 30 minutes, or until meat is tender.
5 Spoon *Barley Pilaf* onto a heated deep serving platter; garnish each kebab with a crab apple and arrange over pilaf.

Barley Pilaf
Fluffy and mildly seasoned, it takes the place of the potato of the meal
Makes 6 servings

1 cup regular barley (from a 1-pound package)
1 large onion, chopped (1 cup)
4 tablespoons (½ stick) butter or margarine
1 envelope instant chicken broth

1 Cook barley in a large amount of boiling salted water in a kettle 1 hour, or just until tender; drain.
2 Sauté onion in butter or margarine until soft in a large frying pan; stir in chicken broth. Add barley; toss to mix well; cover.
3 Heat *very slowly* 15 minutes, or until heated through.

Curried Pork Kebabs, piquant with soy sauce and curry.

Economical and enormously adaptable, pork is prepared here the Korean way with vegetables and a soy-curry sauce.

Penny-Wise Pork Platter
Sweet smoky shoulder or cottage roll, plus three vegetables, make this main course
Makes 4 servings

1 smoked boneless shoulder butt or cottage roll (about 2 pounds)
4 cups water
1 large onion, chopped (1 cup)
6 whole cloves
1 bay leaf
4 large potatoes, pared and quartered
1 pound Brussels sprouts, washed and trimmed OR: 1 package (10 ounces) frozen Brussels sprouts
6 medium-size carrots, scraped and cut into 2-inch pieces
Raisin Sauce (recipe follows)

1 Place meat, water, onion, cloves, and bay leaf in a kettle; cover. Simmer 1 hour.
2 Measure out 1 cup of the liquid for cooking vegetables in next step; continue cooking meat 30 minutes longer, or until tender.
3 While meat cooks, combine potatoes, Brussels sprouts, and carrots with the 1 cup liquid diluted with ½ cup water, in a large saucepan; cover. Cook 25 minutes, or until tender; drain.
4 Lift meat from broth, saving 1 cup of the broth; place meat on a heated serving platter. Arrange vegetables around edge; keep hot while making sauce.
5 Cut meat into ¼-inch-thick slices; serve sauce separately.

RAISIN SAUCE—Combine 3 tablespoons brown sugar, 1 tablespoon cornstarch, ⅛ teaspoon cinnamon, and ⅛ teaspoon ground allspice in a small saucepan; stir in the 1 cup broth (from cooking meat), 1 tablespoon bottled lemon juice, and ¼ cup seedless raisins. Cook, stirring constantly, until sauce thickens and boils 3 minutes; stir in 1 tablespoon butter or margarine until melted. Serve hot. Makes 1½ cups.

Veal Ragout
Long slow cooking in an herb broth gives thrifty breast of veal a superb flavor
Makes 6 servings

3 pounds breast of veal
2 teaspoons salt
4 peppercorns
3 whole cloves
½ teaspoon leaf rosemary, crumbled
Few sprigs parsley
1 clove garlic
4 cups water
1 pound small white onions, peeled
1 can (10½ ounces) condensed cream of mushroom soup
1 slice white bread, toasted and cut in small cubes

1 Have meatman crack breast of veal into 2-inch-long pieces. When ready to cook, cut apart into pieces of 2 ribs each. Place in a kettle or Dutch oven. Add salt, peppercorns, cloves, rosemary, parsley, garlic, and water. Heat to boiling; cover.
2 Simmer 2 hours; place onions on top of meat; cover again. Simmer 1 hour longer, or until meat separates easily from bone. Remove meat and onions with a slotted spoon to a heated shallow serving bowl; keep warm.
3 Strain liquid from kettle into a bowl; measure 1⅓ cups and return to kettle; save remaining to make gravy another day. Stir mushroom soup into kettle; heat to boiling.
4 Spoon over veal. Garnish with toast cubes

and chopped parsley, and sprinkle onions with paprika, if you wish.

Korean Pork Platter

Soy-curry sauce seasons fork-tender meat and four colorful, crisply cooked vegetables
Makes 6 servings

1½ pounds lean boneless pork shoulder, cut in 1-inch cubes
2 tablespoons flour
4 tablespoons vegetable oil
3 teaspoons curry powder
1 tablespoon sugar
⅓ cup soy sauce
¾ cup water
2 large onions, peeled, sliced, and separated in rings
2 cups sliced celery
1 package (9 ounces) frozen cut green beans
2 medium-size yellow squashes, trimmed, halved lengthwise, and sliced
1 teaspoon celery salt

1 Shake pork cubes with flour in a paper bag to coat evenly.
2 Brown in 2 tablespoons of the vegetable oil in a large frying pan; remove and set aside.
3 Stir curry powder into drippings in frying pan; cook 3 minutes. Stir in sugar, soy sauce, and ½ cup of the water; cook, stirring constantly and scraping cooked-on juices from bottom and side of pan, until bubbly; stir in pork; cover.
4 Simmer 1 hour and 15 minutes, or until pork is tender.
5 While meat cooks, sauté onion rings in remaining 2 tablespoons vegetable oil 3 minutes in a second large frying pan; push to one side. Stir in celery; cook 3 minutes. Stir in green beans and squashes. Sprinkle with celery salt; toss to mix; add remaining ¼ cup water; cover.
6 Steam 10 minutes, or until vegetables are crisply tender; drain.
7 Spoon vegetables onto a heated large platter; spoon pork on top.

Oxtail Ragout

If you've never cooked this economical meat, do try it in this succulent stew
Makes 6 servings

Two ragouts, easy to eat and easy on the budget: Veal Ragout and an Oxtail Ragout containing acorn squash.

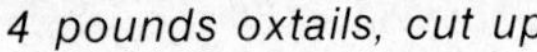

4 pounds oxtails, cut up
2 teaspoons salt
1 teaspoon garlic salt
1 teaspoon sugar
¼ teaspoon pepper
6 whole cloves
1 bay leaf
1 envelope instant beef broth
OR: 1 beef-flavor bouillon cube
1 cup tomato juice
1 cup water
1 package (1 pound) carrots
6 medium-size onions
2 small acorn squashes

1 Brown oxtails in their own fat in a kettle or Dutch oven.
2 Stir in salt, garlic salt, sugar, pepper, cloves, bay leaf, beef broth or bouillon cube, tomato juice, and water; heat to boiling; cover.
3 Simmer 2½ hours, or until meat is almost tender.
4 While meat cooks, pare carrots and cut diagonally in 2-inch lengths. Peel onions and halve. Trim squashes; halve and scoop out seeds, then slice ½ inch thick.
5 Place carrots and onions around meat in kettle; arrange squashes on top; cover again.
6 Simmer 1 hour longer, or until meat separates easily from bone and vegetables are tender. Spoon onto a heated deep serving platter; strain juices from kettle over all.

Barbecued Lamb Riblets

Always popular. And meaty breast of lamb gives you a lot for little
Bake at 350° for 1 hour and 45 minutes. Makes 6 servings

6 pounds breast of lamb
⅓ cup tomato sauce (from an 8-ounce can)
⅓ cup molasses
⅓ cup prepared mustard

1 Trim any excess fat from lamb; cut lamb, if needed, into finger-size pieces of one or two ribs each. Place in a single layer in a jelly-roll pan.
2 Bake in moderate oven (350°) 45 minutes; pour all fat from pan.
3 Mix tomato sauce, molasses, and mustard in a cup; brush part over ribs to coat well.
4 Continue baking, turning once or twice and brushing every 15 minutes with remaining sauce, 1 hour, or until meat is tender and brown.

Old English Chicken Dinner

To make the most of your budget, watch for a sale on chickens, then buy them whole and cut them up yourself
Bake at 400° for 45 minutes. Makes 6 servings

2 broiler-fryers, weighing about 2½ pounds each, cut up
½ cup sifted all-purpose flour
2 teaspoons salt
2 teaspoons paprika
1 teaspoon mixed salad herbs
¼ teaspoon pepper
¼ cup vegetable shortening
Yorkshire Pudding Batter (recipe follows)
1 tablespoon butter or margarine
Giblet Gravy (recipe follows)

1 Wash chicken pieces; set giblets aside for making gravy. Shake chicken pieces, a few at a time, with flour, salt, paprika, salad herbs, and pepper in a paper bag.
2 Brown slowly, turning once, in shortening in two medium-size frying pans, 30 minutes. (Chicken should be crisp, golden brown, and almost tender.)
3 While chicken cooks, make *Yorkshire Pudding Batter*.
4 Melt butter or margarine in a jelly-roll pan, 15x10x1, in oven; pour batter into hot pan; arrange chicken in a single layer in batter. (Pour all drippings into one frying pan; set aside for gravy.)
5 Bake in hot oven (400°) 45 minutes, or until puffed and golden. Cut into squares or oblongs between chicken pieces and lift onto heated plates. Top with *Giblet Gravy*.

YORKSHIRE PUDDING BATTER—Beat 2 eggs slightly with a rotary beater in a medium-size bowl; add 1 cup skim milk, 1 cup sifted all-purpose flour, and ½ teaspoon salt. Beat briskly ½ minute; scrape down side of bowl; beat 1½ minutes longer. (Batter will be smooth and thin.)

GIBLET GRAVY—Slice giblets very thin. Sauté slowly in chicken drippings, stirring often, 15 minutes. Blend in 4 tablespoons flour and 1 teaspoon salt; cook, stirring constantly, until bubbly. Stir in 1½ cups water and 1 cup skim milk; continue cooking and stirring until gravy thickens and boils 1 minute. (If you prefer gravy thinner, stir in another ¼ cup water.)

Beef and Kidney Pie

Meat and vegetables bake lazily in a pastry jacket. Pastry calls for bacon drippings to cut the cost, yet add extra flavor

Bake at 400° for 1 hour and 10 minutes. Makes 6 servings

6 lamb kidneys (about 12 ounces)
1 pound lean boneless beef chuck
Instant unseasoned meat tenderizer
Savory Pastry (recipe follows)
4 medium-size potatoes, pared and sliced thin (3 cups)
1 large onion, peeled and sliced
3 tablespoons flour
1 teaspoon salt
½ teaspoon leaf thyme, crumbled
Dash of ground allspice
¾ cup water
1 teaspoon Worcestershire sauce

1 Soak kidneys overnight in lightly salted water to cover; drain. Halve lengthwise; cut out tubes and white membrane. (Scissors do a neat quick job.) Dice meat.
2 Trim any excess fat from beef; moisten meat and sprinkle with tenderizer, following label directions; cut meat into ½-inch cubes.
3 Try out enough fat trimmings to make 2 tablespoons drippings in a medium-size frying pan; discard trimmings.
4 Brown beef cubes in drippings in frying pan; remove with a slotted spoon and set aside. Sauté kidneys in drippings in same pan, stirring often, just until meat loses its pink color; remove and combine with beef.
5 Prepare *Savory Pastry.* Roll out two thirds to a 12-inch round on a lightly floured pastry cloth or board; fit into a deep 9-inch pie plate; trim overhang to ½ inch.
6 Combine potatoes and onion in a medium-size bowl; sprinkle with flour, salt, thyme, and allspice; toss to coat well. Layer half of the vegetable mixture, all of the meat, and remaining vegetable mixture into prepared pastry shell. Mix water and Worcestershire sauce in a cup; drizzle over filling.
7 Roll out remaining pastry to an 11-inch round; cut several slits near center to let steam escape; cover pie. Trim overhang to 1 inch; turn edges under, flush with rim; flute.
8 Bake in hot oven (400°) 1 hour and 10 minutes, or until meat and vegetables are tender and pastry is richly golden. Let stand 15 minutes, then cut into wedges.

SAVORY PASTRY—Measure 2 cups sifted all-purpose flour into a medium-size bowl; cut in ½ cup chilled bacon drippings with a pastry blender until mixture is crumbly. Sprinkle with 5 tablespoons water, 1 tablespoon at a time; mix lightly with a fork just until pastry holds together and leaves side of bowl clean. (If you do not have bacon drippings, use ⅔ cup vegetable shortening plus ½ teaspoon salt.)

French Steakettes

Makes 6 servings

1 cup dry red wine
1 small onion, peeled and sliced thin
1 tablespoon chopped parsley
1 small clove of garlic, minced
1 small bay leaf
¼ teaspoon leaf thyme, crumbled
2 pounds ground beef
1½ teaspoons salt
Dash of pepper
1 can (about 11 ounces) beef gravy
1 loaf French bread
4 tablespoons (½ stick) butter or margarine

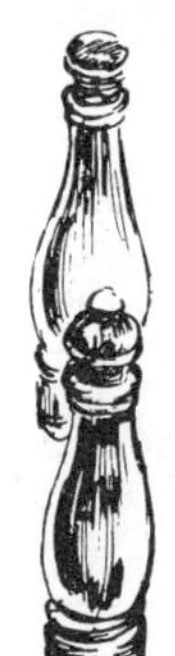

1 Mix wine, onion, parsley, garlic, bay leaf, and thyme in a shallow glass or pottery dish.
2 Mix ground beef lightly with salt and pepper; shape into 6 oval patties about ¾ inch thick. Place in wine mixture in dish. Chill, turning patties carefully several times, at least 3 hours to season.
3 Lift patties from marinade, discarding any onion clinging to meat; place patties on rack in broiler pan. Strain marinade into a small saucepan. Cook rapidly until liquid measures about ⅓ cup; stir in beef gravy; heat until bubbly. Keep hot while fixing bread and cooking meat.
4 Cut bread diagonally into 6 half-inch-thick slices. Spread butter or margarine on both sides.
5 Broil meat patties, 4 to 5 inches from heat, 6 minutes; turn. Broil 2 minutes; place bread on rack beside patties. Continue broiling 2 minutes longer for medium, or until beef is as done as you like it and bread is toasted on both sides.
6 Place bread on heated serving plates; top each slice with a meat patty. Spoon some of the gravy over each, then serve remainder separately so everyone can add more to taste.

Budget Beef Wellington

Bake at 375° for 50 minutes, then at 425° for 25 minutes. Makes 8 servings

2 pounds meat-loaf mixture (ground beef, pork, and veal)

3 eggs
¼ cup fine dry bread crumbs
¼ cup chopped parsley
1 small onion, chopped (¼ cup)
1 can (3 or 4 ounces) sliced mushrooms
1 tablespoon prepared horseradish
2 teaspoons salt
¼ teaspoon pepper
1 package piecrust mix
3 slices process American cheese (from an 8-ounce package)
Herb Gravy (recipe follows)

1 Line a jelly-roll pan with foil.
2 Combine meat-loaf mixture, 2 of the eggs, bread crumbs, parsley, onion, mushrooms and liquid, horseradish, salt, and pepper in a large bowl; mix lightly until well-blended. Shape into an oval loaf, 10x4, in prepared pan.
3 Bake in moderate oven (375°) 50 minutes. Spoon all drippings from pan; cool loaf while making pastry. Raise oven temperature to hot (425°).
4 Prepare piecrust mix, following label directions, or make pastry from your favorite two-crust recipe. Roll out to a rectangle, about 16x13, on a lightly floured pastry cloth or board; trim edges to make a rectangle, 14x12. Cut off a triangular piece, about 1 inch deep, across each corner. (This eliminates thick ends when pastry is wrapped around loaf.) Set all pastry trimmings aside.
5 Place cheese slices, side by side, down center of pastry rectangle; place meat loaf, rounded side down, over cheese.
6 Beat remaining egg with 1 teaspoon water in a cup. Brush part over one long side of pastry, then wrap the two long sides up and over loaf to cover; press edges together to seal.
7 Brush ends of pastry with egg mixture; fold over loaf; press to seal. Place loaf, seam side down, on a greased cooky sheet. Brush all over with egg mixture.
8 Reroll pastry trimmings ⅛ inch thick; cut into ¼-inch-wide strips with a pastry wheel or knife. Press over loaf in a crisscross pattern; brush with egg mixture.
9 Bake in hot oven (425°) 25 minutes, or until pastry is golden. Lift loaf onto a heated serving platter. Garnish with tiny pimiento hearts, if you wish. Cut into thick slices; serve with *Herb Gravy.*

HERB GRAVY—Combine 2 sliced green onions, 1 small bay leaf, and 2 tablespoons butter or margarine in a small frying pan; sauté until onions are soft. Blend in 2 tablespoons flour; cook, stirring constantly, until bubbly. Stir in 1 can (10½ ounces) condensed beef broth. Continue cooking and stirring until mixture thickens and boils 1 minute; remove bay leaf. Stir in 2 tablespoons dry red wine. Makes about 1¼ cups.

Cassoulet
Bake at 350° for 1 hour. Makes 8 servings

1 package (1 pound) dried large lima beans
8 cups water
3 teaspoons salt
6 slices bacon, diced
1 package (8 ounces) heat-and-serve sausages, sliced
1½ pounds ground lamb
2 cans (1 pound each) stewed tomatoes
1 jar (about 8 ounces) junior carrots
2 tablespoons instant minced onion
1 teaspoon leaf thyme, crumbled
1 bay leaf
2 tablespoons chopped parsley

1 Pick over beans. Combine with water and 2 teaspoons of the salt in a kettle; heat to boiling. Cook 2 minutes; cover. Remove from heat and let stand for 1 hour.
2 Heat to boiling again, then simmer 2 hours, or until beans are tender; drain. Spoon into a 12-cup baking dish.
3 Sauté bacon until crisp in a medium-size frying pan; remove with a slotted spoon and add to beans. Add sausages to drippings in pan; brown lightly; combine with bean mixture.
4 Shape lamb into a large patty. Place in same frying pan and brown 5 minutes on each side, then break up into chunks; remove with a slotted spoon to baking dish.
5 Stir in tomatoes, carrots, onion, thyme, bay leaf, and remaining 1 teaspoon salt; toss lightly to mix.
6 Bake, uncovered, in moderate oven (350°) 1 hour, or until bubbly in center; remove bay leaf. Sprinkle with parsley before serving.

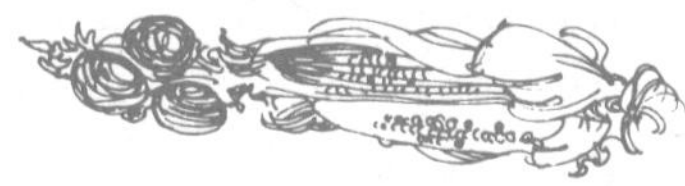

Chinese Pepper Steaks
Makes 6 servings

1 envelope instant beef broth
OR: 1 teaspoon granulated beef bouillon
¼ cup boiling water
2 pounds ground beef
1 tablespoon vegetable oil

1 large green pepper, halved, seeded, and sliced
¾ cup thinly sliced celery
¼ cup sliced green onions
1 can (1 pound) tomatoes
2 tablespoons cornstarch
2 tablespoons soy sauce
Hot cooked rice

1 Dissolve beef broth in boiling water in a cup; stir lightly into ground beef in a large bowl. Shape into 6 patties about 1 inch thick.
2 Brown in vegetable oil, turning once, in a large frying pan; remove with a slotted spoon and place in a shallow pan.
3 Stir green pepper; celery, and green onions into drippings in pan; sauté until soft. Stir in tomatoes; place beef patties in sauce; cover. Simmer 20 minutes. Place patties on a heated deep serving platter.
4 Blend cornstarch with soy sauce and a little water to a paste in a cup; stir into mixture in pan. Cook, stirring constantly, until sauce thickens and boils 3 minutes. Pour over beef patties. Serve over rice.

Polynesian Party Platter
Makes 8 servings

2 cups uncooked regular rice
½ cup thinly sliced celery
1 three-pound canned pork picnic shoulder
¼ cup unsifted all-purpose flour
1 teaspoon ground ginger
5 tablespoons butter or margarine
1 can (1 pound, 4 ounces) pineapple chunks in juice
¼ cup cornstarch
½ cup water
¼ cup firmly packed light brown sugar
¼ cup cider vinegar
¼ cup light molasses
1 can (about 15 ounces) sliced small tomatoes
1 can (1 pound) Italian green beans

1 Combine rice and celery; cook, following label directions for rice; keep warm.
2 Scrape gelatin coating from pork into a small bowl. Cut pork into 1-inch cubes, discarding any fat.
3 Shake pork in a mixture of flour and ginger in a plastic bag to coat evenly.
4 Sauté in 4 tablespoons of the butter or margarine until crusty-brown in a large frying pan; remove with a slotted spoon; keep warm.
5 Drain juice from pineapple into frying pan. Smooth cornstarch and water to a paste in a cup; stir into frying pan, then stir in brown sugar, vinegar, molasses, and gelatin from pork. Cook, stirring constantly, until mixture thickens and boils 3 minutes; add pineapple and pork. Heat until bubbly.
6 Heat tomatoes and beans in their liquids to boiling in separate small saucepans.
7 When ready to serve, spoon rice mixture into an oval or ring on a large serving platter; pile pork mixture in center. Drain liquids from tomatoes and beans; spoon part of each at ends of meat. Season vegetables with remaining 1 tablespoon butter or margarine and sprinkle lightly with salt and pepper. Garnish with green-pepper rings, if you wish.

Ham, apples and "sweets" team in Dixie Ham Dinner.

Dixie Ham Dinner
Bake at 350° for 45 minutes. Makes 8 servings

1 two-pound canned ham
2 cans (1 pound each) vacuum-pack sweet potatoes
5 tablespoons butter or margarine, melted
1 teaspoon salt
Dash of pepper
1 can (1 pound, 4 ounces) pie-sliced apples, drained
¼ cup sugar
½ cup fine gingersnap crumbs

1 Scrape gelatin coating from ham and save to add to soup. Cut ham in ¼-inch-thick slices; stand part around edge in an 8-cup baking dish; place remainder in bottom.
2 Mash sweet potatoes in a large bowl; stir in 2 tablespoons of the melted butter or margarine, salt, and pepper. Spoon over ham in dish. Ar-

range apple slices over potatoes; sprinkle sugar over apples.
3 Blend gingersnap crumbs and remaining 3 tablespoons melted butter or margarine in a small bowl; sprinkle over apples; cover.
4 Bake in moderate oven (350°) 30 minutes; uncover. Bake 15 minutes longer, or until heated through.

Country-Style Pork Pie

Bake at 400° for 15 minutes. Makes 4 servings

1 small head cabbage (about 1 pound)
4 tablespoons (½ stick) butter or margarine
1 teaspoon salt
¼ teaspoon pepper
4 cups prepared instant mashed potatoes
1 cup diced cooked pork
1 can (about 11 ounces) brown gravy with onions
4 hard-cooked eggs, diced
¼ cup chopped parsley

1 Trim cabbage and shred (you will have about 5 cups). Cook in lightly salted water in a large saucepan for 5 minutes, or just until crisply tender; drain well. Toss with 2 tablespoons of the butter or margarine, salt, and pepper.
2 Fold prepared potatoes into cabbage. Spoon over bottom and sides of a buttered shallow 8-cup baking dish.
3 Melt remaining 2 tablespoons butter or margarine in a small skillet; sauté pork 1 minute; add gravy; heat to boiling; remove from heat. Carefully mix in eggs and parsley. Spoon into potato-lined dish.
4 Bake in hot oven (400°) for 15 minutes, or until bubbly-hot.

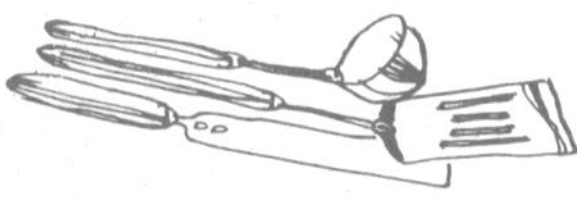

Chicken Risotto

Bake at 400° for 15 minutes. Makes 4 servings

1 cup regular uncooked rice
1 cup sliced celery
1 package (10 ounces) frozen green peas
2 cups water (for rice)
2 teaspoons salt
2 tablespoons butter or margarine
1 cup diced cooked chicken
2 tablespoons flour
⅛ teaspoon pepper
1 small can evaporated milk (⅔ cup)
1⅓ cups water (for sauce)
4 slices process American cheese (4 ounces)
Paprika

1 Combine rice, celery, peas, the 2 cups water, and 1 teaspoon salt in a medium-size saucepan; heat to bubbling; cover; simmer 12 minutes, or until water is absorbed and rice is tender.
2 Melt butter or margarine in a small saucepan; sauté chicken 1 minute; stir in flour, pepper, and remaining 1 teaspoon salt; cook, stirring constantly, just until bubbly. Stir in milk and the 1⅓ cups water; continue cooking and stirring until sauce thickens and boils 1 minute.
3 Pour sauce over rice mixture and toss to combine. Spoon into a buttered shallow 8-cup baking dish. Cut cheese into strips and place in single layer over chicken mixture.
4 Bake in hot oven (400°) for 15 minutes, or until cheese melts and mixture is bubbly-hot. Sprinkle lightly with paprika.

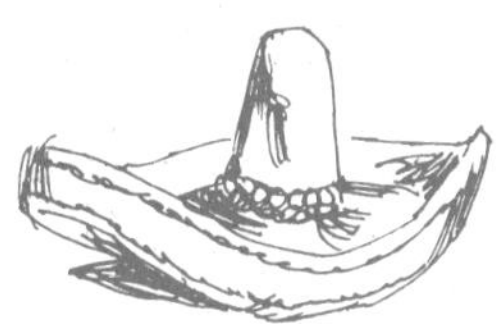

Mexican Hash

Makes 4 servings

2 large onions, chopped (2 cups)
¼ cup bacon drippings
OR: ¼ cup (½ stick) butter or margarine
1 cup finely diced cooked beef
2 teaspoons chili powder
1½ teaspoons salt
¼ teaspoon pepper
Cooked Kidney Beans (recipe follows)
2 cups shredded lettuce (half a head)

1 Sauté chopped onions in bacon drippings or butter or margarine in a large skillet 5 minutes, stirring occasionally; add beef, chili powder, salt, and pepper; cook 1 minute; add *Cooked Kidney Beans;* mix well.
2 Cook slowly for 15 minutes, turning occasionally to blend in any crisp crust.
3 To serve, spoon into deep platter; top with shredded lettuce piled in a mound in center.

COOKED KIDNEY BEANS—Soak 1 pound dry red kidney beans in water to cover overnight in a large bowl; drain. Combine beans, 6 cups cold water, and 3 teaspoons salt in a large saucepan, heat to bubbling; cover; lower heat. Simmer 1½ hours, or until beans are very soft; drain. Mash beans with potato masher or with cooking fork.

Stuffed Cabbage

Fill the leaves with a ground-lamb stuffing, reshape into a head, and steam—that's the secret to this favorite with a twist
Makes 4 generous servings

- *1 small head cabbage (about 1 pound)*
- *4 medium-size potatoes, pared and cubed (3 cups)*
- *1 egg*
- *1 pound ground lamb*
- *1 teaspoon salt*
- *¼ teaspoon pepper*
- *3 tablespoons catsup*
- *1 small onion, chopped (¼ cup)*
- *¼ cup chopped celery*
- *6 tablespoons chopped parsley*
- *1 cup coarse soft bread crumbs (2 slices)*
- *2 tablespoons flour*
- *1½ cups water*

1 Trim cabbage and core. Place head in a kettle of boiling water; cover; remove from heat. Let stand 5 minutes to soften leaves. Lift out head; drain well; let cool and make stuffing.

2 Cook potatoes in boiling salted water in a medium-size saucepan 15 minutes, or until tender; drain. Return to saucepan; mash, then beat in egg.

3 While potatoes cook, brown lamb in a medium-size frying pan 5 minutes on each side, then break up into chunks; continue cooking until no pink color remains. Remove meat with a slotted spoon to a large bowl; stir in salt, pepper, and 1 tablespoon of the catsup.

4 Stir onion and celery into drippings in frying pan; sauté slowly until soft. Remove with a slotted spoon and add to meat mixture. Pour off drippings, then measure 2 tablespoonfuls and return to pan. Set aside for Step 9.

5 Stir 4 tablespoons of the parsley, bread crumbs, and potato mixture into meat mixture.

6 Carefully peel off large cabbage leaves, one by one, leaving small center ones intact for a base; lay large leaves flat on counter top; place center ones upright on a plate for easy handling.

7 Spread a generous spoonful of the meat mixture on each large leaf, then carefully press back around center to reshape head. (Filling will hold them in place.) Spoon any remaining meat mixture in center. Lift head onto a large piece of cheesecloth; fold corners up over top.

8 Set cabbage on a rack or trivet in a kettle; pour in boiling water almost to bottom of rack; cover tightly. Steam 30 minutes, or until cabbage is crisply tender.

9 While cabbage steams, stir flour into drippings in frying pan from Step 4; cook, stirring constantly, just until bubbly. Stir in the 1½ cups water and remaining 2 tablespoons catsup; continue cooking and stirring until gravy thickens and boils 1 minute; stir in remaining 2 tablespoons parsley.

10 Lift cabbage from kettle, holding over kettle a few seconds to let any excess liquid drain off; set on a heated deep serving platter; gently pull out cheesecloth. Garnish platter with parsley and radish roses, if you wish. Cut cabbage into quarters with a sharp knife; serve gravy in a separate bowl to spoon over top.

Budget priced but beautiful, blossom-like head of cabbage stuffed with a savory lamb and crumb stuffing.

Genoese Rice Balls

Pungent salami and Parmesan cheese blend with rice for these bargain-best treats
Makes 4 servings

1 cup uncooked rice
1 package (6 ounces) sliced salami, chopped coarsely
2 eggs, separated
1 can (8 ounces) tomato sauce
3 tablespoons grated Parmesan cheese
½ cup fine dry bread crumbs
Vegetable oil
½ teaspoon leaf basil, crumbled

1 Cook rice, following label directions. Fold in salami, egg yolks, 2 tablespoons of the tomato sauce, and Parmesan cheese. Shape into 12 balls, using about ¼ cup for each.
2 Beat egg whites slightly in a pie plate; place bread crumbs in a second pie plate. Gently roll rice balls in egg white, then in bread crumbs to coat evenly. Chill several hours, or until firm.
3 Pour enough vegetable oil into a small heavy saucepan to make a 3-inch depth; heat to 375°.
4 Fry rice balls, 2 or 3 at a time, turning once, about 4 minutes, or until golden. Lift out with a slotted spoon; drain on paper toweling; keep warm.
5 While rice balls cook, combine remaining tomato sauce with basil in a small saucepan heat slowly, stirring once or twice, until bubbly.
6 Arrange rice balls on a heated deep platter; spoon sauce over all.

Eggplant Parmigiana

Bake at 375° for 20 minutes. Makes 6 servings

1 large eggplant, weighing about 2 pounds
4 tablespoons vegetable oil
1 pound ground beef
2 cloves of garlic, crushed
1 can (about 1 pound) tomatoes
1 can (6 ounces) tomato paste
1 teaspoon salt
¼ teaspoon pepper
1½ cups fresh bread crumbs (3 slices)
⅓ cup grated Parmesan cheese
3 long slices mozzarella cheese
Parsley

1 Trim ends from eggplant; halve lengthwise. Hollow out insides, leaving shells about ¼ inch thick. Cut insides into ½-inch cubes. Place shells in a shallow baking pan and set aside.
2 Sauté eggplant in vegetable oil until soft in a large frying pan; remove with a slotted spoon and drain on paper toweling.
3 Shape ground beef into a large patty in same pan; brown 5 minutes on each side, then break up into small chunks; push to one side. Stir garlic into pan, sauté until soft. Stir in tomatoes, tomato paste, salt, and pepper. Simmer, stirring several times, 15 minutes. Stir in bread crumbs, Parmesan cheese, and eggplant. Spoon into eggplant shells.
4 Cut mozzarella cheese into small triangles; arrange over meat mixture.
5 Bake in moderate oven (375°) 20 minutes or until cheese melts.
6 Line a large platter with buttered green beans, if you wish. Place stuffed eggplant on top; garnish platter with parsley. To serve, cut each half eggplant into thirds with a sharp knife.

Cobbled Beef Ramekins

Cupboard and refrigerator thrifties—corned beef, corn, and biscuits—team up for these savory little casseroles
Bake at 400° for 10 minutes. Makes 4 servings

1 large onion, chopped (1 cup)
2 tablespoons vegetable oil
1 can (12 ounces) corned beef
1 can (8 ounces) cream-style corn
1 teaspoon dry mustard
½ teaspoon leaf sage, crumbled
1 package refrigerated plain or buttermilk biscuits

1 Sauté onion in vegetable oil until soft in a large frying pan; push to one side.
2 Cut corned beef into ½-inch cubes. (Tip: If you chill meat first, it cuts perfectly without crumbling.) Brown cubes lightly in same frying pan; lightly stir in corn, mustard, and sage; cover. Simmer 10 minutes. Spoon into 4 individual baking dishes.
3 Separate the 10 biscuits; cut each of 3 into quarters. Roll each quarter into a small ball with palms of hands; place 3 in center of each baking dish. (Bake remaining biscuits on a cooky sheet along with casseroles and serve separately.)
4 Bake casseroles in hot oven (400°) 10 minutes, or until biscuits are golden. Garnish with strips of pimiento, if you wish.

Fisherman's Platter

Delicate lemon sauce accents poached fish fillets and colorful vegetables
Makes 4 servings

1 package (1 pound) frozen flounder fillets
3 cups water
1 teaspoon salt
3 peppercorns
Few celery tops

Rice is so very versatile. Here it's cooked, teamed with salami and cheese, shaped into balls and fried.

New way with an old favorite, Eggplant Parmigiana—with the meaty tomato sauce baked in eggplant shells.

1 onion slice
1 lemon slice
4 tablespoons (½ stick) butter or margarine
4 tablespoons flour
1 teaspoon lemon juice
1 package (10 ounces) frozen mixed vegetables, cooked and drained

1 Thaw fish and separate carefully into fillets.
2 Combine water with salt, peppercorns, celery tops, and onion and lemon slices in a large frying pan; heat to boiling. Place fillets in pan; cover. Simmer 7 minutes, or until fish flakes easily; lift out carefully with a wide spatula; keep warm.
3 Reheat fish liquid to boiling; cook rapidly until reduced to 2 cups; strain into a 2-cup measure.
4 Melt butter or margarine in same frying pan; stir in flour; cook, stirring constantly, just until bubbly. Stir in the 2 cups fish liquid; continue cooking and stirring until sauce thickens and boils 1 minute; remove from heat. Stir in lemon juice and a drop of food coloring to tint yellow, if you wish.
5 Spoon some of the cooked vegetables onto a heated shallow serving platter; lay fish fillets, overlapping, on top; spoon remaining vegetables over fish. Top fish with several spoonfuls of the sauce; serve remaining separately.

Salmon Crêpes
Bake at 400° for 10 minutes. Makes 6 servings, 2 crêpes each

¾ cup sifted all-purpose flour (for crêpes)
¾ teaspoon salt
2 eggs
1 cup milk
4 tablespoons (½ stick) butter or margarine (for crêpes and sauce)
Butter or margarine for frying
3 tablespoons flour (for sauce)
Dash of pepper
¼ teaspoon leaf tarragon, crumbled
1½ cups light cream or table cream
2 egg yolks, slightly beaten
1 can (1 pound) salmon, drained, boned, and flaked
1 tablespoon freeze-dried chives
1 tablespoon lemon juice
3 tablespoons grated Parmesan cheese

1 Combine the ¾ cup flour and ¼ teaspoon of the salt in a medium-size bowl. Beat eggs until blended in a small bowl; stir in milk; beat into flour mixture until smooth. Melt 1 tablespoon of the butter or margarine in a small saucepan; stir into batter. Cover; chill 2 hours.
2 Heat a 7-inch frying pan slowly; test temperature by sprinkling in a few drops of water. When drops bounce about, temperature is right. Grease pan lightly with butter or margarine.
3 Measure batter, 2 tablespoonfuls at a time, into pan, tilting pan to cover bottom. (To speed measuring, use your ¼ cup measure and fill half full.) Bake crêpe 1 to 2 minutes, or until bottom browns; turn; bake 1 minute longer. As crêpes are baked, stack on a plate with paper toweling between; keep warm. Repeat with remaining batter, buttering pan before each baking, to make 12 crêpes.
4 Melt remaining 3 tablespoons butter or margarine in a medium-size saucepan; blend in the 3 tablespoons flour. Cook, stirring constantly, until bubbly. Stir in remaining ½ teaspoon salt, pepper, tarragon, and cream. Continue cooking and stirring until sauce thickens and boils 1 minute.
5 Beat egg yolks slightly in a small bowl; stir in about half of the hot sauce, then stir back into remaining sauce in pan. Cook 1 minute longer; remove from heat.
6 Blend ¾ cup of the sauce with salmon and chives in a medium-size bowl; stir lemon juice into remaining sauce.
7 Place a heaping tablespoon of the salmon mixture on each crêpe; roll up, jelly-roll fashion; place in a single layer in a buttered broilerproof dish, 13x9x2. Pour remaining sauce over crêpes; sprinkle Parmesan cheese over all.
8 Bake in hot oven (400°) 10 minutes, or until bubbly. (If you prefer top slightly brown, place in broiler for 2 to 3 minutes.) Serve hot.

Polynesian Tuna
Makes 6 servings

1 small green pepper, halved, seeded, and cut in strips
1 medium-size onion, peeled and sliced
1 tablespoon butter or margarine
1 can (5 ounces) water chestnuts, drained and sliced
1 can (3 or 4 ounces) sliced mushrooms
½ teaspoon ground ginger
¼ teaspoon pepper
2 envelopes instant chicken broth or 2 teaspoons granulated chicken bouillon
1½ cups water
2 cans (about 7 ounces each) tuna, drained and broken in chunks
1 package (7 ounces) frozen Chinese pea pods
4 teaspoons cornstarch
¼ cup diced pimientos
1 can (3 ounces) Chinese fried noodles

1 Sauté green pepper and onion in butter or

As economical as it is quick: Cobbled Beef Ramekins.

Polynesian Tuna, tossed together in just 10 minutes is a beautiful budget-stretcher even though it contains Deluxe Chinese snow pea pods.

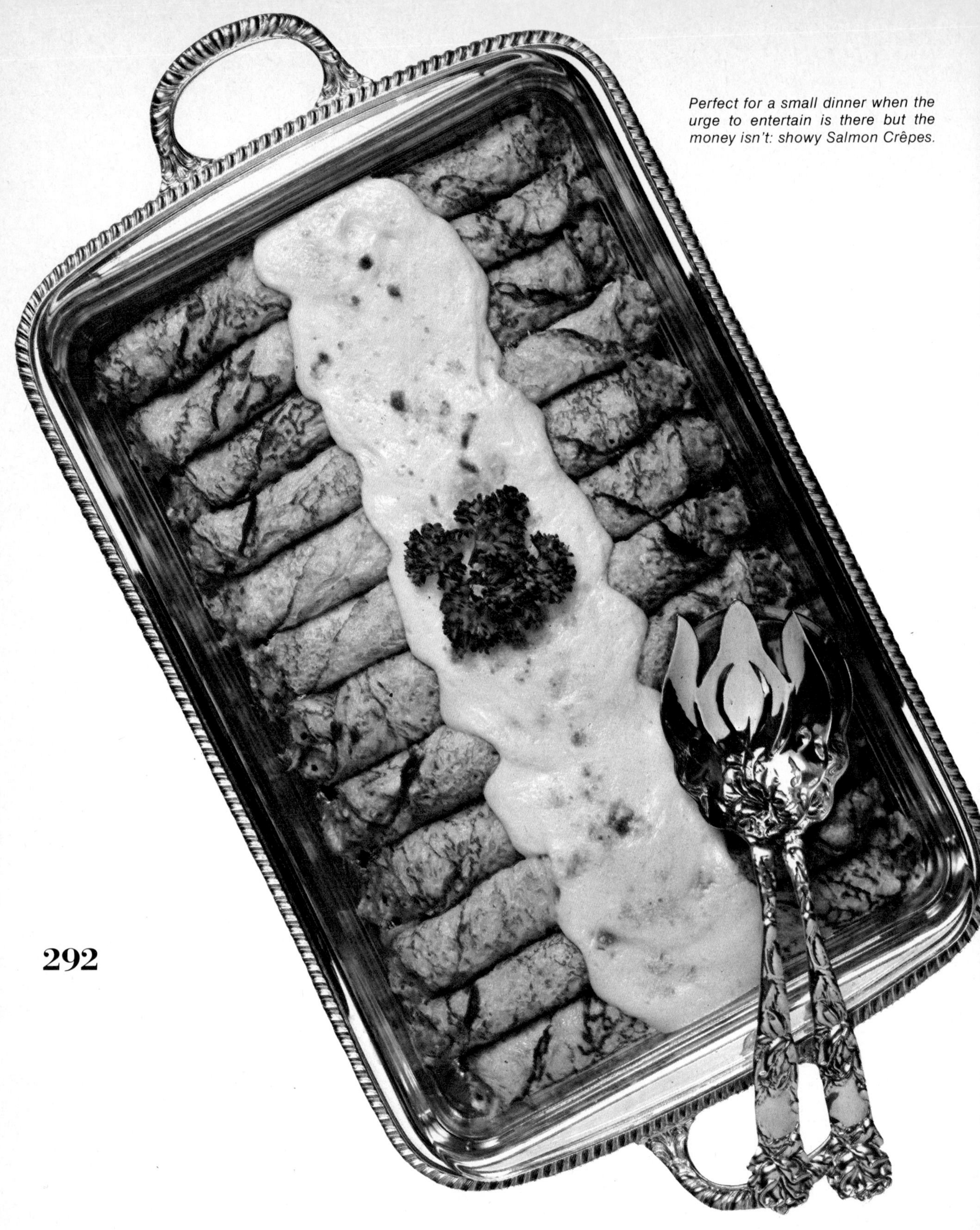

Perfect for a small dinner when the urge to entertain is there but the money isn't: showy Salmon Crêpes.

margarine until soft in a large frying pan. Stir in water chestnuts, mushrooms and liquid, ginger, pepper, chicken broth, and water.
2 Heat slowly to boiling. Add tuna and pea pods; cover. Simmer 4 minutes.
3 Smooth cornstarch with a little water to a paste in a cup; stir into tuna mixture. Cook, stirring carefully, until sauce thickens and boils 3 minutes; stir in pimientos.
4 Spoon tuna mixture in center of a deep platter or shallow dish; place noodles around edge.

SIX SAVORY MEAT-STRETCHERS

Shredded Chicken and Vegetables
Makes 4 servings

1 chicken breast (14 ounces), split, skinned and boned
2 tablespoons vegetable oil
1 clove of garlic, minced
3 carrots, thinly sliced
2 small zucchini, sliced
1 cup frozen sliced green beans
6 water chestnuts
2 teaspoons salt
⅛ teaspoon pepper
3 tablespoons soy sauce
1 cup water
1 tablespoon cornstarch
1 tablespoon dry sherry (optional)
2 cups hot cooked rice
2 tablespoons toasted sliced almonds (optional)

1 Cut chicken into thin shreds. Heat oil in a large skillet. Add chicken; quickly stir-fry until the color turns from pink to white, about 3 minutes.
2 Add garlic, carrots, zucchini, beans, water chestnuts, salt, pepper, soy sauce and ¾ cup of the water. Cover; reduce heat; simmer until vegetables are crisply tender, about 5 minutes (do not overcook vegetables).
3 Combine cornstarch, sherry and remaining ¼ cup of the water in a cup. Add to skillet; cook and stir gently just until sauce is thickened and bubbly. Spoon hot rice onto serving platter; spoon mixture over; sprinkle with almonds.

Swiss Ham and Vegetable Skillet Meal
Makes 4 servings

1 large onion, sliced
¼ cup (½ stick) butter or margarine
1 pound cooked ham, finely chopped
2 pounds potatoes, peeled and cut into ½-inch cubes
½ teaspoon salt
⅛ teaspoon pepper
½ teaspoon leaf rosemary, crumbled
1 tablespoon flour
1 envelope instant beef broth
1 cup water
1 package (10 ounces) frozen peas

1 Sauté onion in butter or margarine until golden in a large skillet. Add the ham; cook, stirring constantly, 3 minutes longer. Add potatoes; sprinkle with salt, pepper, rosemary and flour.
2 Combine instant beef broth with water; pour over top. Bring to boiling; reduce heat; cover; simmer until potatoes are almost done, 10 minutes.
3 Add peas; cook until peas and potatoes are tender, about 15 minutes longer.

Shredded Beef and Vegetables
Makes 4 servings

1 pound boneless sirloin or round steak
3 tablespoons vegetable oil
2 cloves of garlic, chopped
½ small head of cauliflower, broken into flowerettes
1 green pepper, seeded and cut into strips
3 carrots, thinly sliced
1 can (1 pound) bean sprouts, drained
4 water chestnuts, thinly sliced (optional)
½ teaspoon ground ginger
⅓ cup soy sauce
1 cup water
1 tablespoon cornstarch
2 cups hot cooked rice

1 Cut meat in very thin strips across the grain. Sauté in hot oil in a large skillet 3 minutes over high heat, turning to brown; remove; keep warm.
2 Add garlic, cauliflower, pepper and carrots. Cook, stirring constantly, until vegetables are crisply tender, about 3 minutes. Add bean sprouts, water chestnuts, ginger, soy sauce and water. Cook, covered, 5 minutes longer; add meat.
3 Blend cornstarch with 2 tablespoons water in a cup; add to skillet. Cook 1 minute, or until thickened and bubbly. Serve over rice.

Some cake, Country Omelet Cake! Puffy layers of omelet filled with budget-priced corned beef hash.

Country Omelet Cake
Bake at 350° for 20 minutes. Makes 6 servings

8 eggs, separated
¾ cup water
3 tablespoons flour
½ teaspoon seasoned salt
Few drops liquid red pepper seasoning
1 medium-size onion, chopped (½ cup)
2 tablespoons butter or margarine
1 can (1 pound) corned-beef hash
1 can (10¾ ounces) condensed tomato soup

1 Generously grease 2 eight-inch round layer-cake pans.
2 Beat egg whites until foamy-white and double in volume in a large bowl. Add 3 tablespoons of the water; continue beating until whites stand in firm peaks.
3 Beat egg yolks with flour, salt, and red-pepper seasoning until creamy-thick in a medium-size bowl; fold into beaten egg whites until no streaks of yellow remain. Pour evenly into prepared pans.
4 Bake in moderate oven (350°) 20 minutes, or until puffed and firm.
5 While omelets bake, sauté onion in butter or margarine until soft in a medium-size frying pan; stir in corned-beef hash. Heat slowly until hot. Blend tomato soup and remaining water in a small saucepan; heat to boiling.
6 Loosen one omelet layer around edge with a knife; carefully turn out onto a heated serving plate; spread corned-beef hash mixture over top. Loosen second layer; remove from pan; place over hash layer. Spoon part of the tomato sauce over omelet; cut into wedges. Serve at once with remaining tomato sauce.

Spicy Lamb Casserole
Makes 6 servings

2 pounds lean boneless lamb
3 tablespoons butter or margarine
1 large onion, sliced
2 cloves of garlic, minced
2 tablespoons flour
1½ cups water
2 envelopes instant beef broth
½ teaspoon ground cinnamon
½ teaspoon ground ginger
½ teaspoon ground cardamom
⅔ cup golden raisins
1 teaspoon salt
⅛ teaspoon pepper
3 small yellow squashes, cubed
¼ cup lemon juice

1 Cut meat into 2-inch strips. Sauté in butter or margarine until brown in a large skillet; transfer to a 10-cup baking dish.
2 Sauté the onion and garlic in the remaining fat until soft. Stir in the flour, water, beef broth, cinnamon, ginger, cardamom, raisins, salt and pepper. Cook, stirring constantly, 2 minutes.
3 Pour the sauce over the meat. Simmer, covered, for 35 minutes, or until meat is almost tender. Add the squash and lemon juice; continue cooking until squash is tender, about 15 minutes.

Potato Moussaka
Makes 6 servings

3 medium-size onions, chopped
6 tablespoons (¾ stick) butter or margarine
1 pound ground beef or lamb
2 tablespoons minced parsley
½ teaspoon ground thyme
2 teaspoons salt
⅛ teaspoon freshly ground pepper
2 tablespoons flour
¼ cup water
3 eggs
1 cup light cream or milk
2 pounds potatoes, sliced
¼ cup fine dry bread crumbs

1 Sauté the onions in 2 tablespoons of the butter or margarine until soft in a large skillet. Add the meat; cook, stirring constantly, 3 minutes longer. Stir in parsley, thyme, salt, pepper and 1 tablespoon of the flour. Add the water. Cook, stirring constantly, for 2 minutes, or until thickened. Remove from heat; cool.
2 Separate 2 of the eggs; beat yolks with 2 tablespoons of the cream or milk in a small bowl. Stir into the meat mixture. Beat the whites of the 2 eggs until stiff in a small bowl; fold into the meat mixture.
3 Heat 3 tablespoons of the butter or margarine in a large skillet. Add the potatoes; cook, covered, stirring several times until half done.
4 Butter a 10-cup baking dish with remaining butter or margarine; sprinkle with bread crumbs. Layer meat and potatoes in baking dish, ending with potatoes. Bake, uncovered, in moderate oven (350°) for 30 minutes.
5 Beat the remaining flour, cream or milk and egg together in a small bowl; pour over top of potatoes. Bake 10 minutes longer.

SOME MEAT-STRETCHING SECRETS

Nothing stretches the food budget more effectively than making a little meat go a long way. Here are some sure-fire ways to do it:

- Put potatoes, pasta, legumes and whole grains to good use. They're budget priced, nutritious and pair happily with most cuts of meat.
- Scrutinize your favorite casserole recipes. Can you reduce the quantity of meat in them? *Slightly?* Chances are you can, cutting costs but not the quality of the casserole.
- Substitute meat drippings, rendered chicken fat for the more expensive butter and margarine. They've excellent flavor (*except* for lamb and mutton drippings, which are both strong-flavored and difficult to digest).
- Substitute vegetable cooking water, broths and bouillons for water in soups, stews and casseroles. And add a hearty seasoning of herbs. Gives a robust character to mini-meated recipes.
- Bolster meat-stretched recipes with sensational salads or vegetables. And accompany with husky peasant breads.

Cajun Shrimp Stew (recipe in Vol. 1)

BURGER BONANZA

BURGER BONANZA: MEAT LOAVES, BURGERS, TOPPERS AND SPREADS, CASSEROLES AND SKILLET DINNERS

Few meats are more versatile than ground meats. Or more economical (there's no bone so they're all edible). Ground meat should not be taken to be synonymous with ground beef—ground lamb, veal, pork and ham are all equally available and appealing, though each, because there's less demand for it, must be ground to order.

Ground beef, of course, is the all-American favorite. Many a supermarket, in fact, builds its reputation around its ground beef, grinding it fresh each day—often several times a day, when the store is at its busiest—so whether you pick up a package labeled "regular ground beef," "ground chuck," "ground round" or "meat-loaf mixture" (combinations of beef and pork or beef, pork and veal), you can be certain the meat is today's offering.

What to do with ground meat? Meat loaves, to be sure. And burgers with dozens of flavor variations. And meat balls swimming in savory sauce or gravy. And flavorful casseroles with a foreign accent. And quick skillet dinners. And meat pies. And . . . the list is long and alluring as the following collection of recipes proves. But first, some tips on buying and storing the different kinds of ground meats.

The makings of a magnificent meat loaf: ground beef chuck, chopped yellow onion, garlic, pepper and herbs.

HOW TO BUY GROUND MEAT

Your supermarket displays are bountiful, and, depending on the cut and kind of meat used, the cost will vary. Here are descriptions of the choices, with reasons why their price tags vary.

1 REGULAR GROUND BEEF—Freshly ground beef made from lean meat and fat as cut from a whole side of beef. You can recognize it by its speckled pink and white color, and its good beef flavor makes it an all-round favorite for hamburger patties, casseroles, meat loaves, and sauces. To speed shopping, this popular budget-tagged grind is wrapped in 1-, 2-, and 3-pound packs, often with a "special" price on the 3-pounders.

2 GROUND BEEF CHUCK—Its name describes it, for only flavorful chuck is used. Its pink meatiness has just enough fat to give it juicy goodness. Sold mostly in about 1-pound packages, this grind, too, is a perfect choice for all-round hamburger needs.

3 GROUND BEEF ROUND—This is de luxe "hamburger" with a price tag to match its quality. Your supermarket grinds it from lean beef round, which gives it its rich red color. Like ground chuck, it is sold mostly in about-1-pound packs, or you can ask your meatman to grind any amount you want to your order.

4 GROUND VEAL—Shoulder, shank, neck, flank and breast are the cuts to have ground. Shoulder is the most expensive and, gourmets insist, the most flavorful and succulent. The other cuts are sinewy (grinding renders them

Regular Ground Beef: economical, casserole-perfect.

Ground Chuck: lean, moderately priced, multi-purposed.

Ground Round: very lean, expensive as "hamburger" goes.

tender and juicy) *and* economical. Veal by itself is too lean to make juicy loaves or patties so should be mixed about half and half with ground beef, pork, lamb or sausage meat.

5 GROUND LAMB—Shoulder is the choicest cut to grind because it contains just the proper proportion of fat, has excellent texture and flavor. But neck and shank are good for grinding, too.

6 GROUND FRESH PORK—Shoulder, picnic or lean trimmings from the side or belly make the best ground pork. *Warning:* All fresh pork—and that includes any meat-loaf mixture containing fresh ground pork—must be cooked until well done (internal temperature of 185° F.) because of the danger of trichinosis (a disease caused by the small parasite present in some fresh pork). Thorough cooking makes pork safe to eat.

7 GROUND COOKED HAM—You can, of course, grind your own ham leftovers and you'll save money by doing so. Or you can have the butcher grind cooked ready-to-eat ham. For mellower flavor, ground ham is often combined about two-to-one or half and half with ground fresh pork, veal or beef.

8 MEAT-LOAF MIXTURES—When a recipe suggests a mixture such as ground beef and pork or ground beef, pork, and veal, ask your meatman to grind it to your order, or pick up a package packed in any of these ways: (1) Each meat ground separately and displayed in a single package as ground beef and pork, or ground beef, pork, and veal; (2) Ground meats already blended and labeled MEAT LOAF.

The most-popular-weight package is about 2 pounds—1½ pounds ground beef to ½ pound ground pork for beef-pork mix and 1¼ pounds ground beef to 6 ounces each ground pork and veal for the three-meat combination. Either choice is enough to make a 6-to-8-serving meat loaf.

SOME TIPS FOR CALORIE-COUNTERS:

Despite its higher price, the leanest chopped meat is your best buy. A four-ounce portion of chopped sirloin is around 220 calories; chopped round, 223 calories; bottom round, 343 calories; and chopped chuck 292 calories. These are average cuts of meat and the assumption is that no extra fat has been added. Beef fat weighs in at 204 calories per ounce, so a four-ounce hamburger that's half fat can be easily as high as 500 calories. Of course, some of the fat cooks away . . . some of it doesn't. A bad bargain both ways.

Pick out a lean piece of beef: Sirloin, flank, round . . . even chuck if it seems lean, or at least trimmable of fat (fat around the edges, not all through it). Develop an "eye" for leanness and you'll be able to spot calorie bargains in the lower-priced cuts.

Have the butcher whack away every last scrap of fat and then grind up the lean.

Try veal loaf for a change; it's lower in calories. Or a blend of two parts beef to one part veal. But watch out for those prepackaged beef-veal-pork "meat-loaf blends"; they're apt to be the most calorific of all.

ODD WEIGHTS NEEDN'T CONFUSE YOU

In shopping for the meat you need, you are likely to find packages labeled slightly under or over even weights. And for a very good reason. Meatmen are good guessers of the weights needed, so they watch the meat as it comes from the grinder, and divide it into mounds. With no further handling, each mound is weighed automatically and marked with its exact ounce weight. Buy the weight nearest to the amount you need for your recipe, for any slightly over or under ounces will make no difference.

YOUR MEATMAN EXPLAINS "BLOOM"

If you open a package of rich red ground meat only to find the meat darker on the inside, you needn't be concerned about its freshness. This change in color—"bloom" your meatman calls it—is natural because much of the air has been closed out of the package. Leave the meat unwrapped in the refrigerator for a short time and its bright color will "bloom" again.

HOW TO STORE GROUND MEAT

To use the same day or the next: Tear off a corner of the transparent covering to expose the meat to the air, or remove wrapper entirely and rewrap meat loosely in wax paper or foil. Store in the meat-keeper or coldest part of your refrigerator.

To freeze ground meat for patties: Shape meat lightly into patties, preferably plain, as seasoning flavors tend to build during freezing. Wrap patties in freezer paper, foil, transparent wrap or bags and seal tightly. For single servings, wrap each patty separately. For family servings, stack three, four, or more patties with double-thick wax paper or foil between, then wrap and seal. Come cooking time, patties are easy to separate.

Want a bagful for a cookout or party? Arrange

Meat-Loaf Mixture: about 2 parts beef, 1 part pork.

Meat-Loaf Mixture: ½ beef, ¼ each pork and veal.

Premixed Meat-Loaf Mixture, usually a beef-pork mix.

patties, without touching, on a cooky sheet, then fast-freeze in the coldest part of the freezer. When frozen, pile into a transparent bag and seal. You can take out as many as you need at a time, reseal the bag, and return the rest

to the freezer. Be sure to label all packages with the contents and the date, and plan to use within four months.

MEAT LOAVES

Country Beef Loaf

Bake at 350° for 1 hour. Makes 8 servings

2 tablespoons butter or margarine
½ pound mushrooms, trimmed and sliced
1 large onion, diced (1 cup)
1 cup thinly sliced celery
1 cup shredded pared carrots
2 tablespoons water
2 pounds ground beef
½ cup sifted all-purpose flour
2 teaspoons salt
1 teaspoon seasoned salt
1 teaspoon fines herbes
2 tablespoons soy sauce

1 Combine butter or margarine, mushrooms, onion, celery, carrots, and water in a medium-size frying pan; heat to boiling; cover. Cook 10 minutes, or until vegetables are crisply tender.
2 Combine ground beef, flour, salt, seasoned salt, fines herbes, soy sauce, and cooked vegetable mixture in a large bowl; mix lightly until well-blended. Shape into a rectangular loaf, 8x6, in a greased jelly-roll pan.
3 Bake in moderate oven (350°) 1 hour, or until crusty-brown. Sprinkle with chopped parsley before serving, if you wish.

Old-Fashioned Sage Loaf

Bake at 350° for 1 hour and 15 minutes. Makes 8 servings

2 pounds meat-loaf mixture (ground beef and pork)
2 eggs
1 cup quick-cooking rolled oats
1 medium-size onion, grated
1 cup canned applesauce
2 teaspoons salt
¼ teaspoon pepper
½ teaspoon leaf sage, crumbled
1 tablespoon bottled steak sauce

1 Mix meat-loaf mixture lightly with eggs, rolled oats, onion, applesauce, salt, pepper, and sage until well-blended.
2 Pack firmly into a loaf pan, 9x5x3; unmold into a shallow baking pan. Score top in criss-cross pattern; brush with steak sauce.
3 Bake in moderate oven (350°) 1 hour and 15 minutes, or until brown.

Variation:

PICNIC SQUARES—Prepare and bake *Old-Fashioned Sage Loaf,* following directions above, then chill. (A day ahead is best.) Cut lengthwise into 2 long blocks, then crosswise into ½-inch-thick slices; wrap each block tightly in foil to carry to your picnic spot. Just before serving, spread split soft rolls generously with bottled mustard-dressing sauce; put together sandwich style, with sliced meat loaf. Each block of meat loaf will cut into about 16 slices.

Cooksaver tip:

It's a good idea to remove the hot meat juices and drippings from the baking pan before unmolding meat loaf. A baster does a fast neat job, or you can use a small spoon. Make the drippings into gravy or save to use as a base

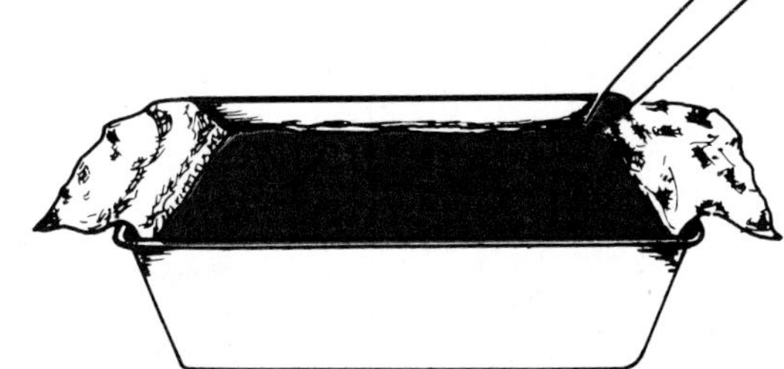

A big ham loaf, dome-shaped, glazed and clove-studded.

for soup another day. And for easier unmolding—dishwashing, too—line the bottom and ends of the baking pan with a strip of foil.

●

Saucy Meat Loaf

Bake at 375° about 45 minutes. Makes 6 servings

1 medium-size onion, sliced
1½ pounds ground beef
½ teaspoon salt
½ teaspoon basil
¼ teaspoon leaf oregano, crumbled
1 can (10¾ ounces) condensed tomato soup

1 Save 3 or 4 onion rings for topping; place the rest in the bottom of a baking pan, 8x8x2; cover onions with ground beef; break up lightly with a fork, but do not pack down; sprinkle with salt, basil, and oregano; top with saved onion rings; pour tomato soup over.
2 Bake in moderate oven (375°) 45 minutes, or until done as you like it. Meat forms a tasty loaf with rich gravy around it.

Cooksaver tip:

To have plenty for seconds when serving a crowd, or an on-hand treat to slice cold for sandwiches, mix a double batch of meat loaf and bake as "twins." Saves time and dishwashing—and oven heat too.

Deviled Meat Loaf

Bake at 350° for 1 hour. Makes 8 servings

2 pounds ground beef
1 can (4½ ounces) deviled ham
¾ cup chopped parsley
½ cup fine dry bread crumbs
1 egg
1 small onion, grated
2 teaspoons salt
2 teaspoons leaf basil, crumbled
⅛ teaspoon pepper
1 cup tomato juice

1 Mix ground beef and deviled ham lightly with remaining ingredients until well-blended; shape into a loaf in a shallow baking pan.
2 Bake in moderate oven (350°) 1 hour, or until brown.

●

Charcoal-Grilled Beefburger Roll-Up

It's a prize-winning recipe and perfect for a party. See if it doesn't win you
Makes 6 servings

1½ pounds ground beef
2 cups coarse bread crumbs (4 slices)
½ cup evaporated milk
1 medium-size onion, chopped (½ cup)
1 cup green olives, chopped
1 clove of garlic, minced
2 eggs
1 teaspoon salt
½ teaspoon paprika
¼ teaspoon pepper
½ cup bottled barbecue sauce

1 Combine all ingredients except barbecue sauce, in large bowl; mix lightly with a fork until well-blended.
2 Shape meat into a 12-inch-long roll on a sheet of heavy foil; wrap tightly and seal lengthwise with a drugstore fold. Fold one end over and over to seal; stand roll on end; tap gently to settle meat; seal other end. (This much can be done early in the day and roll chilled until cooking time.)
3 To grill: Take roll from refrigerator when you start fire. When coals are white-hot, place roll in its foil cover on grill. Grill, turning roll a quarter turn every 10 minutes, for 40 minutes.
4 Slide roll far enough from heat to unwrap; open foil and crush it around roll to form a cooking pan. Brush roll generously with barbecue sauce. Continue grilling, turning and brushing often with sauce, until meat is richly browned and done as you like it.
5 Cut into thick slices; serve as part of a dinner plate, or make into jumbo sandwiches with buttered, toasted hamburger buns.

Beef 'n' Apricot Pinwheel Loaf

Tangy apricot stuffing whirls round and round inside a savory ground-beef jacket
Bake at 350° for 1 hour. Makes 6 servings

½ cup chopped dried apricots
½ cup water
1½ pounds ground beef
½ pound ground veal
2 tablespoons chopped parsley
1 egg
¼ cup dairy sour cream
1 teaspoon salt (for meat)
⅛ teaspoon pepper
2 cups ready-mix bread stuffing (half an 8-ounce package)
¼ cup chopped celery
2 tablespoons melted butter or margarine
¼ teaspoon salt (for stuffing)
Dash of pepper
4 slices bacon

1 Simmer apricots in water in medium-size saucepan 1 minute; remove from heat.
2 Combine beef, veal, parsley, egg, sour cream, salt, and pepper in large bowl; mix lightly. Pat into a rectangle, 10x8, on sheet of wax paper or foil.
3 Stir bread stuffing, celery, butter or margarine, salt, and pepper into apricots in saucepan;

Jumbo-sized, juicy meat-loaf dressed for the table with a wreath of halved cherry tomatoes, snowy cauliflowerets.

spread evenly over meat; roll up jelly-roll fashion; pinch together at ends to seal.
4 Place roll in greased shallow baking pan; lay bacon slices over top.
5 Bake in moderate oven (350°) 1 hour, or until richly browned.

Early Harvest Meat Loaf

Bake at 350° for 50 minutes. Makes 6 servings

1½ pounds ground beef
¾ cup fine dry bread crumbs
¾ cup canned applesauce
6 tablespoons catsup
¾ teaspoon salt
¼ teaspoon leaf sage, crumbled

1 Combine all ingredients in large bowl; mix lightly with fork; shape into a 6-inch square in baking pan.
2 Bake in moderate oven (350°) 50 minutes, or until done as you like it.
3 Place on heated platter to cut and serve in squares.

Ham-and-Cheese Meat Loaf

Bake at 350° for 1 hour. Makes 8 servings

2 pounds meat-loaf mixture (ground beef and pork)
1 small can evaporated milk (⅔ cup)
2 eggs, beaten
1½ cups soft bread crumbs (3 slices)
2 tablespoons grated onion
2 tablespoons prepared mustard
2 teaspoons salt
1 package (4 ounces) sliced boiled ham, cut in thin strips
4 slices Swiss cheese, cut in thin strips (from an 8-ounce package)
½ cup bottled barbecue sauce with minced mushroom

1 Combine meat-loaf mixture, milk, eggs, bread crumbs, onion, mustard, and salt in a large bowl. Mix meat mixture (using hands makes it easy) until very smooth.
2 Pack half the meat mixture into an 8-cup baking dish; top with ham and cheese strips to within 1 inch of edge. Pack remaining meat mixture into dish, being sure to cover filling completely. Unmold onto a shallow baking dish.
3 Bake in moderate oven (350°) 50 minutes. Brush barbecue sauce over meat loaf. Bake 10 minutes longer, brushing once with remaining barbecue sauce, or until loaf is a rich brown.

Mini Barbecued Beef Loaves

Makes 6 servings

1½ pounds ground beef
2 tablespoons grated onion
1½ teaspoons salt
⅛ teaspoon pepper
1 cup chili sauce
3 tablespoons brown sugar
1½ teaspoons dry mustard
1½ tablespoons vinegar
2 drops liquid red pepper seasoning

1 Combine beef, onion, salt, and pepper; shape into 6 small loaves.
2 Combine remaining ingredients.
3 Broil loaves with tops 4 inches from heat 5 minutes; turn; spoon sauce over tops; broil 5 to 7 minutes, or until done to your taste.

Twin Meat Loaves

Bake at 375° for 45 minutes. Makes 6 servings

1¾ pounds ground beef
¼ pound sausage meat
1 cup soft bread crumbs (2 slices)
½ cup catsup (for meat)
1 large onion, chopped (1 cup)
1 egg, slightly beaten
2 teaspoons Worcestershire sauce
1½ teaspoons salt
⅛ teaspoon pepper
½ cup catsup (for topping)
1 tablespoon brown sugar
¼ teaspoon dry mustard
Dash of liquid red pepper seasoning

1 Combine beef, sausage meat, bread crumbs, ½ cup catsup, onion, egg, Worcestershire sauce, salt, and pepper in large bowl; blend lightly; form into 2 rectangular loaves in shallow baking pan.
2 Bake in moderate oven (375°) 30 minutes; remove from oven; spread tops of loaves with mixture of ½ cup catsup, brown sugar, mustard, and liquid red pepper seasoning.
3 Return meat to oven; continue to bake, basting once or twice with sauce, 15 minutes, or until tops are bubbly brown. Garnish with green pepper strips, if desired.

Not as complicated as it looks, a checkerboard loaf made of a bread stuffing mix and zippily seasoned ground beef. Shaping trick: keep meat and stuffing mixtures separate, pat each into logs, alternate in loaf pan forming checkerboard.

Checkerboard Beef

This loaf owes its new look and flavor to herb stuffing and a shaping trick
Bake at 375° for 1 hour and 15 minutes. Makes 6 servings

1 package (8 ounces) herb-seasoned ready-mix bread stuffing
Butter or margarine
Water
2 teaspoons grated onion
2 pounds ground beef
1 egg
½ cup chopped celery
2 teaspoons seasoned salt

1 Prepare stuffing mix with butter or margarine and water, following label directions; stir in grated onion.

2 Blend ground beef with egg, celery, and seasoned salt in a large bowl.

3 Press one third of the meat mixture lengthwise into a loaf pan, 9x5x3, to cover half of bottom; press one third of the stuffing mixture in a strip alongside meat. Make two more layers of each, alternating strips of meat and stuffing each time; cover.

4 Bake in moderate oven (375°) 45 minutes; uncover. Bake 30 minutes longer, or until browned. Turn out; let stand 15 minutes for easier slicing.

Here's how to fix Checkerboard Beef

Divide meat and stuffing mixtures into thirds and start building. First pat one third of meat into a strip in pan and one third of stuffing alongside it to make a layer. Continue with two more

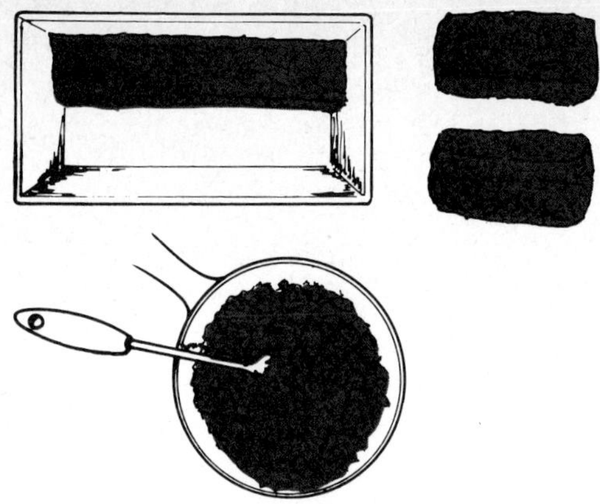

layers, reversing the order each time, to give a checkerboard pattern

Curried Beef Ring

Mold that's baked with the rice inside, plus make-it-yourself fresh chutney
Bake at 350° for 45 minutes. Makes 8 servings

2 pounds ground beef
2 eggs
1 large tart apple, pared, quartered, cored, and diced (1 cup)
½ cup golden raisins
1 teaspoon salt
1 tablespoon lemon juice
1 large onion, chopped (1 cup)
1 clove of garlic, minced
5 tablespoons butter or margarine
1 tablespoon curry powder
¼ teaspoon ground ginger
1 envelope instant chicken broth OR: 1 chicken-bouillon cube
1 cup milk
2 cups cooked rice
Vegetable Chutney (recipe follows)

1 Combine ground beef, eggs, apple, raisins, salt, and lemon juice in a large bowl; mix lightly.
2 Sauté onion and garlic in 4 tablespoons of the butter or margarine until soft in a small frying pan; stir into meat mixture. Heat curry powder in remaining 1 tablespoon butter or margarine in same pan 1 minute; stir in ginger, chicken broth or bouillon cube, and milk, crushing bouillon cube, if used, with a spoon. Stir into meat mixture; fold in cooked rice. Pack into a well-greased 8-cup ring mold.
3 Bake in moderate oven (350°) 45 minutes, or until loaf is crusty-brown and starts to pull away from edge of mold; remove from oven. Let stand 5 minutes, then loosen around outside and center edge with a knife. Cover with a large serving plate; turn both upside down; gently lift off mold. Spoon *Vegetable Chutney* into center.

VEGETABLE CHUTNEY—Peel 1 large onion; slice and separate into rings. Cut 2 medium-size tomatoes into thin wedges. Halve 1 medium-size green pepper; remove seeds; dice pepper. Thinly slice 2 small stalks celery. Melt 4 tablespoons (½ stick) butter or margarine in a large frying pan; stir in vegetables. Heat, tossing lightly several times, 2 to 3 minutes, or just until vegetables wilt; remove from heat. Mix 1 teaspoon sugar, 2 tablespoons lemon juice, and ¼ teaspoon liquid red pepper seasoning in a cup; drizzle over vegetables; toss lightly.

Matambre Roll

This version of a popular way with steak calls for ground beef wrapped around a moist carrot-and-parsley stuffing
Bake at 350° for 1 hour. Makes 8 servings

2 pounds ground beef
1 teaspoon seasoned salt
½ teaspoon seasoned pepper
¼ cup smoke-flavor barbecue sauce
¼ cup catsup
2 cups shredded pared carrots
1 cup soft bread crumbs (2 slices)
½ cup chopped parsley
1 teaspoon salt
2 eggs, beaten
1 cup hot water
¼ cup instant-type flour
1 cup milk

1 Combine ground beef with seasoned salt and pepper in a large bowl; mix lightly with a fork. Pat into a thin rectangle, 14x12, on wax paper. (For easy handling, paper should be a few inches longer than meat layer.)
2 Mix barbecue sauce and catsup in a cup; brush about half over meat layer. (Set remaining aside for Steps 3 and 4.)
3 Mix carrots, bread crumbs, parsley, salt, and eggs in a medium-size bowl; spread evenly over meat. Roll up, jelly-roll fashion, using paper as a guide; lift into a greased large shallow baking pan; remove wax paper. Brush roll all over with part of remaining sauce mixture.
4 Bake in moderate oven (350°), brushing several times with remaining sauce mixture, 1 hour, or until richly glazed. Remove from pan and keep hot while making gravy.
5 Stir water into drippings in pan, scraping any browned bits from bottom of pan. Blend flour and milk in a 2-cup measure; stir into drippings

mixture. Cook, stirring constantly, until gravy thickens and boils 1 minute. Season with salt, if needed. Slice roll and serve with gravy.

Vegetable-Stuffed Beef Roll

Cooked mixed vegetables make the colorful filling of the pinwheel-shape servings
Bake at 375° for 1 hour. Makes 6 servings

1 medium-size onion, chopped (½ cup)
2 tablespoons butter or margarine
1 package (10 ounces) frozen mixed vegetables
2 pounds ground beef
1 egg, beaten
1 tablespoon prepared mustard
2 teaspoons Worcestershire sauce
1 teaspoon salt
¼ teaspoon pepper
1 cup grated process American cheese (4 ounces)
3 slices bacon, cut in half

1 Sauté onion in butter or margarine until soft in a medium-size frying pan; stir in frozen mixed vegetables. Heat over low heat, breaking up vegetables with a fork; cover, then cook 10 minutes, or until almost tender. Drain well; cool while preparing meat.
2 Combine ground beef, egg, mustard, Worcestershire sauce, salt, and pepper in a medium-size bowl; mix with a fork until blended.
3 Pat into a rectangle, 16x10, on wax paper or foil; spread with cooled vegetable mixture to within 1 inch of edges; sprinkle with cheese. Starting at a 10-inch end, roll up, jelly-roll fashion, lifting wax paper or foil as you roll to steady and guide it. Place, seam side down, in a greased large shallow baking pan. Top with bacon slices.
4 Bake in moderate oven (375°) 1 hour, or until a deep brown. Lift onto heated serving platter; cut into ½-inch-thick slices with a sharp knife.

European Pâté Loaf

Twin meat filling, layered with gherkins, bakes in a golden pastry jacket before topping with a zippy jellied bouillon
Bake at 350° for 1 hour and 45 minutes. Makes 6 to 8 servings

1 pound ground veal
1 pound ground beef
2 eggs
1 small onion, grated
1 tablespoon all-purpose flour
2 teaspoons salt
½ teaspoon leaf marjoram, crumbled
¼ teaspoon pepper
2 cans (10½ ounces each) condensed beef broth
Meat-Pie Pastry (recipe follows)
10 small sweet pickles, quartered lengthwise
1 envelope unflavored gelatin

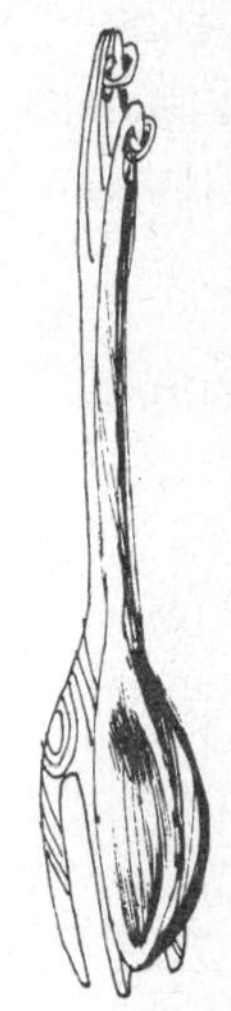

1 Combine ground veal and beef in a large bowl. Beat eggs slightly in a cup; measure 2 tablespoons into a second cup and set aside for brushing loaf in Step 4. Add remaining to meat mixture with onion, flour, salt, marjoram, pepper, and ½ cup of the broth; mix well with a fork. (Set remaining broth aside for Step 6.)
2 Make MEAT-PIE PASTRY. Roll out ⅔ to a rectangle, 15x10, on a lightly floured pastry cloth or board; fit into a loaf pan, 9x5x3.
3 Spoon one third of the meat mixture in an even layer in bottom of pan; place half of the pickle slices lengthwise in five evenly spaced rows on top. Repeat with another layer of each, then top with remaining third of meat mixture. Fold edges of pastry over meat.

4 Roll out remaining pastry to a rectangle, 10x6; trim evenly to 9x5, then cut several slits to let steam escape. Place over meat loaf; pinch edges to seal; brush with saved beaten egg.
5 Bake in moderate oven (350°) 1 hour and 45 minutes, or until golden. (During baking, juices from meat may bubble up around edges and through openings in top but will soak back into loaf as it cools.) Place pan on a wire rack to cool while preparing gelatin mixture.
6 Soften gelatin in ½ cup of the remaining broth in a small saucepan; heat, stirring constantly, over low heat until gelatin dissolves; remove from heat. Stir in remaining broth.
7 Push a skewer through each of the openings in top of loaf, pushing it to bottom of meat, then spoon in just enough of the warm gelatin mixture to fill holes. Let stand until gelatin mixture soaks into meat. Repeat several more times with remaining gelatin mixture until no more will soak into meat. (Save any remaining gelatin mixture to add to soup.) Chill loaf several hours, or even overnight. When ready to serve, cut in thick slices with a sharp knife.

MEAT-PIE PASTRY—Combine 2 cups sifted all-purpose flour and 1 teaspoon salt in a medium-size bowl; cut in ⅔ vegetable shortening with a pastry blender until mixture is crumbly. Sprinkle 4 to 5 tablespoons cold water over, a tablespoon at a time; mix lightly with a fork until pastry holds together and leaves side of bowl clean.

Beef-Macaroni Loaf

Bake at 350° for 1 hour. Makes 6 to 8 servings

Macaroni Layers

1 package (8 ounces) elbow macaroni
2 tablespoons butter or margarine
2 tablespoons flour
1 teaspoon salt
¼ teaspoon pepper
1 egg
2 cups milk
½ cup grated Parmesan cheese

Meat Layer

1 small onion, chopped (¼ cup)
1 tablespoon butter or margarine
1½ pounds ground beef
1 egg
1 can (10¾ ounces) condensed tomato soup
1 teaspoon salt
¼ teaspoon pepper

Sauce

1 can (8 ounces) tomato sauce
1 teaspoon sugar
¼ teaspoon leaf basil, crumbled

1 Grease a loaf pan, 9x5x3; line bottom and ends with a double-thick strip of foil, leaving a 1-inch overhang; grease foil.
2 Make macaroni layers: Cook macaroni, following label directions; drain; return to kettle. Stir in butter or margarine; sprinkle flour, salt, and pepper over; toss to mix well.
3 Beat egg; stir in milk; pour over macaroni mixture. Cook, stirring constantly, over medium heat, until thickened; remove from heat. Stir in Parmesan cheese.
4 Make meat layer: Sauté onion in butter or margarine until soft; add ground beef and brown, breaking meat up with a fork as it cooks.
5 Beat egg; stir in ½ can of the tomato soup, salt, and pepper; stir into cooked meat mixture.
6 Spoon half of the macaroni mixture in an even layer in prepared pan; top with all of the meat mixture, then remaining macaroni mixture.
7 Bake in moderate oven (350°) 1 hour, or until firm and brown on top.
8 Make sauce: While loaf bakes, heat tomato sauce with remaining ½ can of tomato soup, sugar, and basil to boiling; simmer 2 to 3 minutes to blend flavors.
9 Cool loaf in pan 10 minutes; loosen from sides with knife, then lift up ends of foil and set loaf on a heated serving platter; slide out foil. Frame platter and top loaf with steamed green and red pepper rings, if you wish. Slice loaf; serve sauce separately to spoon over.

Planked Beef Dinner

Makes 4 servings

1½ pounds ground beef
Salt
½ teaspoon freshly ground black pepper
2 medium-size tomatoes, halved crosswise
2 tablespoons soft butter or margarine
¼ teaspoon Worcestershire sauce
¼ teaspoon prepared mustard
½ cup soft bread crumbs (1 slice)
1 package (9 ounces) frozen whole green beans
½ cup grated mild Cheddar cheese
2½ cups prepared instant mashed potatoes

1 Mix ground beef slightly with 1½ teaspoons salt; shape into a rectangle, 7x5; press pepper into each side of meat. Place on rack in broiler pan.
2 Broil, 4 to 5 inches from heat, 10 minutes; turn; broil 4 minutes longer. Place on a large ovenproof platter.
3 While meat broils, sprinkle tomato halves lightly with salt. Blend butter or margarine with Worcestershire sauce and mustard in a small bowl; stir in bread crumbs. Spread on tomato halves, dividing evenly.
4 Cook green beans, following label directions; drain; keep hot. Stir cheese into mashed potatoes.
5 Place 2 tomato halves at each end of platter next to meat; spoon potato mixture in a border around edge.
6 Broil, 5 inches from heat, about 5 minutes, or until potatoes and topping on tomatoes are golden. Place platter on a board. Arrange green beans beside meat.

Italian Meat Loaves in Squash Bowls

Herb-and-cheese-sparked ground beef bakes crusty-brown in golden squash halves
Bake at 375° for 1 hour and 45 minutes. Makes 6 servings

Beef-Macaroni Loaf with a high-style layered look.

3 medium-size acorn squashes
2 tablespoons melted butter or margarine
Salt and pepper (for squashes)
1½ pounds ground beef
1½ cups soft bread crumbs (3 slices)
1 egg
⅓ cup catsup
1 teaspoon salt
1 teaspoon leaf oregano, crumbled
2 tablespoons grated Parmesan cheese

1 Halve squashes; scoop out seeds, but do not pare. Brush hollows with melted butter or margarine; sprinkle lightly with salt and pepper.
2 Combine ground beef, bread crumbs, egg, catsup, salt, and oregano in medium-size bowl; mix lightly. Heap into squash halves, dividing evenly. (Mixture will mound well.) Sprinkle with cheese. Stand squashes in shallow baking pan.
3 Bake, uncovered, in moderate oven (375°) 45 minutes. Cover with foil; bake 1 hour longer, or until squashes are tender.

Parisian Meat Loaf Stacks
Makes 8 servings

2 pounds meat-loaf mixture (ground beef, pork, and veal)
1 can (10½ ounces) condensed onion soup
2 tablespoons flour
½ cup water
1 loaf French bread, cut diagonally into 8 thick slices and toasted
Grated Parmesan cheese

1 Shape meat-loaf mixture into a thick 6-inch round; place in a medium-size frying pan. Pour onion soup over top; heat to boiling; cover.
2 Simmer, spooning liquid in pan over meat several times, 1½ hours. Lift patty onto a carving board.
3 Blend flour and water to a paste in a cup; stir into liquid in pan. Cook, stirring constantly, until gravy thickens and boils 1 minute.
4 Place each slice of French bread on a heated serving plate. Slice meat loaf and place on top; spoon gravy over all. Sprinkle each generously with Parmesan cheese.

Dill-Sauced Meat Loaf
Bake at 350° for 1 hour and 15 minutes. Makes 6 servings

1½ pounds meat-loaf mixture (ground beef and pork)
1 medium-size onion, chopped (½ cup)
½ cup soft bread crumbs (1 slice)
½ cup bottled dill-pickle juice
1 egg
1½ teaspoons salt
¼ teaspoon pepper
½ cup chopped dill pickle
½ cup catsup
¼ cup water
2 tablespoons sugar
1 teaspoon Worcestershire sauce

1 Mix meat-loaf mixture lightly with onion, bread crumbs, dill-pickle juice, egg, salt, and pepper until well-blended. Shape into a loaf in a shallow baking pan.
2 Combine dill pickle, catsup, water, sugar, and Worcestershire sauce; pour over loaf.
3 Bake in moderate oven (350°), basting twice with sauce in pan, 40 minutes. Continue baking, without basting, 35 minutes longer, or until richly glazed.

Piquant Ring With Green Rice
Bake at 350° for 1 hour. Makes 10 to 12 servings

3 pounds meat-loaf mixture (ground beef, pork, and veal)
2 cups soft bread crumbs (4 slices)
3 eggs
1 medium-size onion, grated
½ cup milk
¼ cup prepared mustard
2 teaspoons salt
½ teaspoon ground cloves
½ cup firmly packed brown sugar
⅓ cup cider vinegar
¼ cup orange juice
¼ cup molasses
Green Rice (recipe follows)

1 Mix meat-loaf mixture lightly with bread crumbs, eggs, onion, milk, mustard, salt, and cloves until well-blended. Pack into an 8-cup ring mold; unmold into a shallow baking pan.
2 Bake in moderate oven (350°) 30 minutes.
3 While ring bakes, combine brown sugar, vinegar, orange juice, and molasses; cook, stirring often, 10 minutes, or until slightly thick. Spoon part over meat.
4 Continue baking, basting often with remaining glaze, 30 minutes longer, or until richly browned.
5 To serve, place loaf on a heated serving platter; spoon *Green Rice* in center.

GREEN RICE—Combine 1 cup uncooked rice,

Meat-loaves needn't be loaf-shaped —literally. They can be a round or a ring. The two NON-loaf loaves pictured here are dome-shaped Dill-Sauced Meat-Loaf and doughnut-shaped Piquant Ring filled with Green Rice.

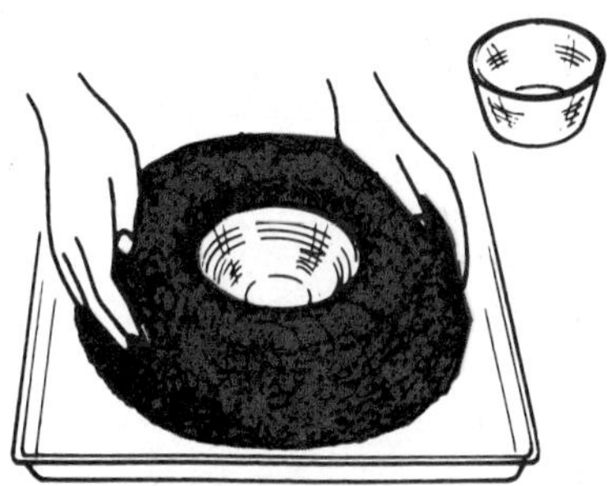

Cooksaver tip:
To give meat loaf a fancy shape, pack mixture into a ring mold, then invert into baking pan.

When baked, fill center of loaf with mashed potatoes or a vegetable. No ring mold? Make your own by molding loaf around a custard cup.

2½ cups water, 2 tablespoons butter or margarine, and 1 teaspoon salt in a 6-cup baking dish; cover. Bake along with meat ring in moderate oven (350°) 1 hour, or until rice is tender and liquid is absorbed. Stir in ½ cup finely chopped celery and ¼ cup chopped parsley. Makes 4 cups.

Mock Pot Roast With Vegetables

Bake at 375° for 1 hour and 15 minutes. Makes 8 servings

2 pounds meat-loaf mixture (ground beef, pork, and veal)
½ cup quick-cooking rolled oats
2 eggs
½ cup catsup
1 tablespoon prepared horseradish
1 teaspoon dry mustard
3 teaspoons salt
¼ teaspoon pepper
1 teaspoon bottled gravy coloring
8 small carrots, pared
8 small potatoes, pared
16 small white onions, peeled
1 package (10 ounces) frozen peas

1 Mix meat-loaf mixture lightly with rolled oats, eggs, catsup, horseradish, mustard, 2 teaspoons of the salt, and pepper until well-blended. Shape into a loaf in a shallow baking pan; brush with gravy coloring.
2 Halve carrots lengthwise; arrange with potatoes and onions around meat; sprinkle with the remaining 1 teaspoon salt. Cover pan with foil.
3 Bake in moderate oven (375°) 40 minutes; uncover; add peas. Cover again; bake 30 minutes. Uncover; baste meat and vegetables with pan juices; bake 5 minutes longer, or until vegetables are tender.

Meat Loaf Finlandia

Bake at 375° for 1 hour. Makes 6 servings

1 medium-size onion, chopped (½ cup)
1 tablespoon butter or margarine
1 pound ground veal
1 pound ground fresh pork
1½ cups soft bread crumbs (3 slices)
1 egg
1 tablespoon chopped parsley
1 teaspoon salt
½ teaspoon crushed fennel seeds
¼ teaspoon pepper
12 dried apricot halves
6 dried pitted prunes
Paprika
1 envelope chicken gravy mix
Water

A veal loaf, made extra juicy with carrot shreds.

For an unusually savory and succulent meat-loaf, pot roast it in the company of potatoes, onions, carrots and green peas. This one is called Mock Pot Roast.

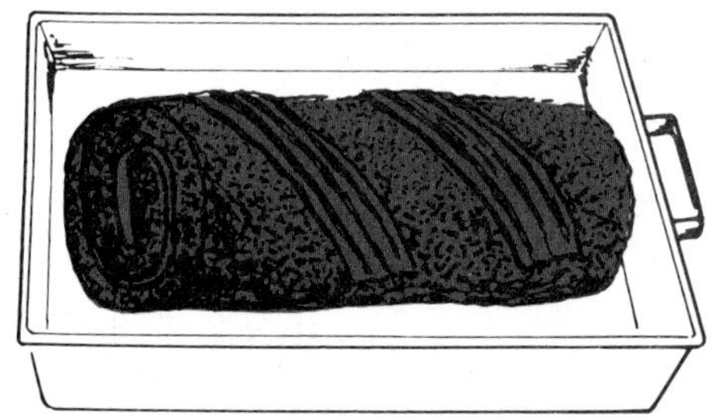

Cooksaver tip:

A few slices of bacon arranged over meat loaf will help to keep it moist during baking and give it extra flavor as well as a pretty top. Another idea: Brush with barbecue sauce.

1 Sauté onion in butter or margarine until soft in a small frying pan; remove from heat.
2 Combine with veal, pork, bread crumbs, egg, parsley, salt, fennel, and pepper in a large bowl; mix lightly until well-blended.
3 Pour boiling water to cover over apricots and prunes in a small bowl; let stand 1 minute; drain.
4 Pat meat mixture into a thin rectangle, 16x10, on waxed paper or foil. Sprinkle generously with paprika.
5 Place 6 of the apricot halves in a row across short end of meat; top each with a prune, then remaining apricot halves. Roll up meat tightly, jelly-roll fashion, using wax paper or foil as a guide. Place, seam side down, in a greased large shallow baking pan.
6 Bake in moderate oven (375°) 1 hour, or until roll is crusty-brown.
7 Prepare chicken gravy mix with water, following label directions. Slice roll crosswise with a sharp knife and serve with gravy.

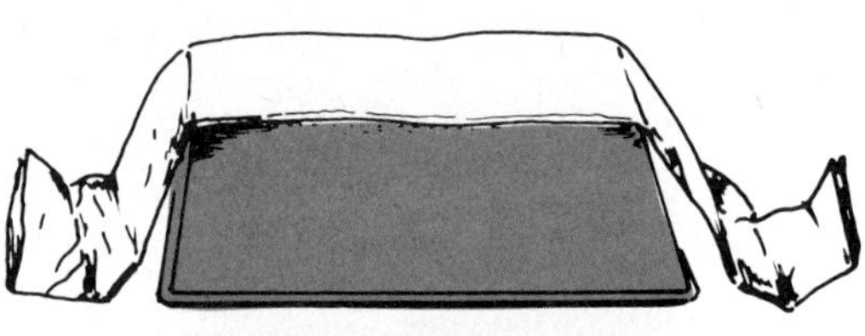

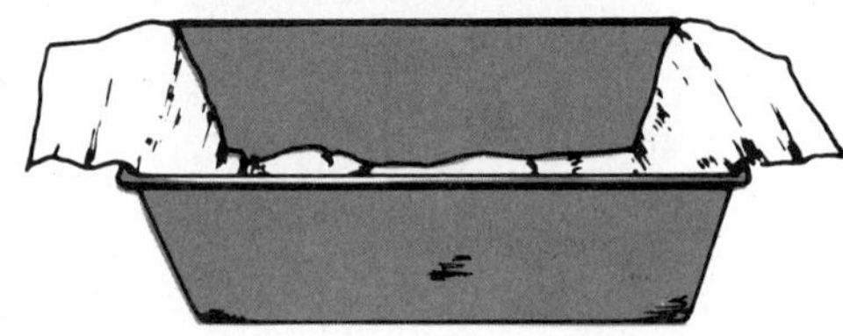

Cooksaver tip:
To line a loaf pan: Fold a double sheet of foil to fit across bottom and up ends of pan with an inch overhang. Flip pan right side up and grease; press the strip inside and grease again.

Autumn Veal Loaf
Bake at 375° for 1¼ hours. Makes 6 servings

1 small acorn squash
1½ pounds ground veal shoulder
1 small onion, chopped (¼ cup)
1 can (3 or 4 ounces) chopped mushrooms
1 cup soft bread crumbs (2 slices)
1 teaspoon salt
¼ teaspoon pepper
1 cup (8-ounce carton) dairy sour cream

1 Cut squash into quarters; remove seeds and strings; pare; grate into large bowl; stir in remaining ingredients; mix lightly just until blended; form into a loaf about 9x5x3 in a greased shallow baking pan.
2 Bake in moderate oven (375°) 1 hour and 15 minutes, or until top is brown.

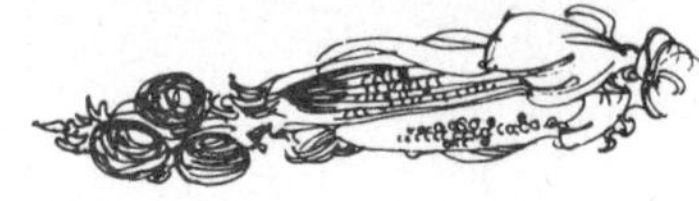

Pimiento Veal Loaf
Bake at 350° for 1 hour and 5 minutes. Makes 8 servings

2 pounds ground veal
1 cup fine dry bread crumbs
½ cup grated Parmesan cheese
1 medium-size onion, chopped (½ cup)
¼ cup chopped pimiento-stuffed olives
1 egg
1½ cups tomato juice
2 tablespoons lemon juice
2 teaspoons salt
½ teaspoon pepper
2 cans or jars (4 ounces each) whole pimientos, drained
4 tablespoons (½ stick) butter or margarine
¼ cup sifted all-purpose flour
1 envelope instant chicken broth
OR: 1 teaspoon granulated chicken bouillon
1 teaspoon salad seasoning
1 cup water
2 tablespoons dry sherry

1 Line a loaf pan, 9x5x3, with foil, leaving a 1-inch overhang all around; grease foil well.
2 Combine veal, bread crumbs, Parmesan cheese, onion, olives, egg, ½ cup of the tomato juice, lemon juice, salt, and pepper in a large bowl; mix lightly until well-blended.
3 Carefully slit each pimiento lengthwise at sides to form two pieces. Place pieces, insides up, over bottom and slightly up sides of pan. (Pimientos should cover entire bottom of pan and form a petal effect on sides.) Gently press meat mixture into pan.
4 Bake in moderate oven (350°) 1 hour and 5 minutes, or until lightly brown on top.
5 Lift up on foil to loosen loaf from pan; cover pan with a heated serving platter. Turn upside down; carefully remove pan and peel off foil.
6 Melt butter or margarine in medium-size saucepan; blend in flour, chicken broth, and salad seasoning. Cook, stirring constantly, until bubbly. Stir in remaining 1 cup tomato juice, water, and sherry; continue cooking and stirring until sauce thickens and boils 1 minute. Slice loaf; serve with sauce.

Gourmet Veal Loaf

Bake at 375° for 1¼ hours. Makes 6 servings

1½ pounds ground veal shoulder
2 cups grated raw carrots
1 small onion, chopped (¼ cup)
1 can (3 to 4 ounces) chopped mushrooms
½ cup fine dry bread crumbs
1 teaspoon salt
¼ teaspoon pepper
1 cup (8-ounce container) dairy sour cream

1 Combine all ingredients in large bowl; mix lightly with fork; spoon into loaf pan, 9x5x3; invert onto shallow pan; carefully remove loaf pan; score top of loaf lightly.
2 Bake in moderate oven (375°) 1 hour and 15 minutes, or until rich golden brown on top.
3 For party serving, place loaf on plank or ovenproof platter; edge with mashed potatoes, and tomato halves brushed with a parsley-butter sauce; broil 10 minutes, or until potatoes are light brown.

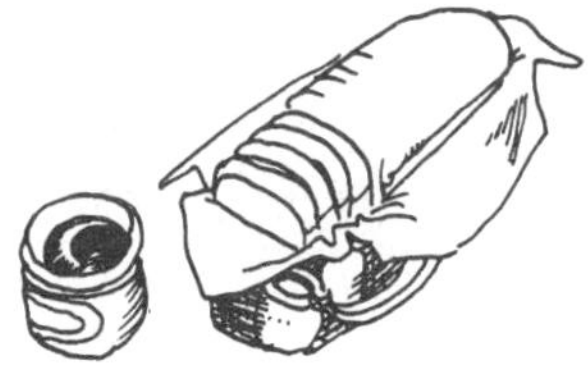

Jumbo Ham Roll

Bits and pieces of ham and kernels of corn go into the filling for this supper loaf that bakes in a biscuit blanket.
Bake at 375° for 40 minutes. Makes 6 to 8 servings

4 cups ground cooked ham (about 2 pounds)
1 can (12 or 16 ounces) whole-kernel corn, drained
1 cup soft bread crumbs (2 slices)
2 eggs
1 teaspoon mixed salad herbs
½ teaspoon dry mustard
⅛ teaspoon pepper
½ cup milk (for filling)
2 cups biscuit mix
⅔ cup milk (for crust)
Parsley Cream Sauce (recipe follows)

1 Combine ham, corn, bread crumbs, eggs, salad herbs, mustard, pepper, and the ½ cup milk in a large bowl; mix lightly with a fork.
2 Prepare biscuit mix with the ⅔ cup milk, following label directions; turn out onto a lightly floured pastry cloth or board. Knead gently ½ minute, then roll out to a rectangle, 18x12. Place on a lightly greased large cookie sheet.
3 Spoon ham filling down middle ⅓ of dough; fold edges up over filling to center; pinch together at top and ends to seal. Cut several slits in top to let steam escape.
4 Bake in moderate oven (375°) 40 minutes, or until crust is golden-brown. Cut in thick slices; serve with PARSLEY CREAM SAUCE.

●

Parsley Cream Sauce

Lots of chopped parsley gives it just the right zip.
Makes about 2 cups

1 small onion, chopped (¼ cup)
4 tablespoons (½ stick) butter or margarine
¼ cup sifted all-purpose flour
½ teaspoon salt
Dash of pepper
2 cups milk
1 envelope instant chicken broth
OR: 1 chicken-bouillon cube
¼ cup chopped parsley

1 Sauté onion in butter or margarine until soft in a medium-size saucepan; stir in flour, salt, and pepper; cook, stirring constantly, just until bubbly. Stir in milk and instant chicken broth or bouillon cube; continue cooking and stirring, crushing bouillon cube, if using, with a spoon, until sauce thickens and boils 1 minute.
2 Before serving, stir in parsley.

●

Veal and Ham Ring

Bake at 350° for 40 minutes. Makes 6 servings

1 pound ground veal shoulder
1 pound ground cooked ham
¼ cup grated American cheese
1 small onion, chopped (¼ cup)
¼ cup fine dry bread crumbs
½ teaspoon salt
¼ teaspoon curry powder
½ cup milk
3 tablespoons honey
1 teaspoon bottled gravy coloring
1 can (1 pound, 2 ounces) sweet potatoes

1 Combine veal, ham, cheese, onion, bread crumbs, salt, curry powder, and milk; mix lightly with fork.
2 Spoon into 8-inch ring mold; invert onto shallow pan; remove mold.
3 Combine honey and gravy coloring in cup; brush half over meat.
4 Bake in moderate oven (350°) about 20 minutes; brush meat with remaining honey mixture; place sweet potatoes in baking pan with meat;

baste with juices in pan; bake 20 minutes longer, or until meat and potatoes are glazed.
5 Place on heated platter; if you wish, fill center of ring with cooked cauliflower topped with buttered bread crumbs and chopped parsley.

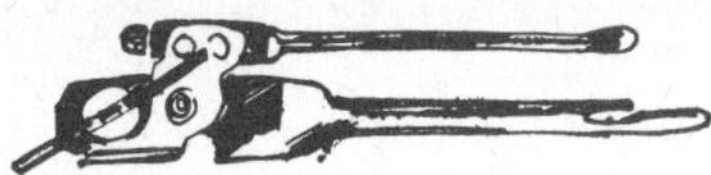

Greek Lamb Loaf

Bake at 350° for 1 hour. Makes 8 servings

1 medium-size onion, chopped (½ cup)
2 tablespoons butter or margarine
½ cup shredded carrot (1 small)
½ cup shredded raw potato (1 small)
1 small eggplant (about 1 pound), trimmed, pared, and shredded (about 2½ cups)
2 cloves of garlic, thinly sliced
2 pounds ground lamb
2 eggs
2 medium-size tomatoes, peeled and finely diced (1 cup)
1½ cups fine dry bread crumbs
3 teaspoons salt
½ teaspoon ground cinnamon
¼ teaspoon pepper
4 tablespoons lemon juice
2 tablespoons sugar

1 Sauté onion in butter or margarine in a medium-size skillet 3 minutes; remove from heat; stir in carrot, potato, eggplant, and garlic, tossing to coat well; cover. Cook 5 minutes, or until wilted but still crisp.
2 Combine ground lamb, eggs, tomatoes, bread crumbs, salt, cinnamon, pepper, 2 tablespoons of the lemon juice, and the cooked vegetables in a large bowl, mixing lightly. Press firmly into a 9x5x3-inch loaf pan. Turn out onto a lightly greased large shallow baking pan.
3 Bake in moderate oven (350°) 45 minutes. Mix remaining 2 tablespoons lemon juice and sugar in a cup, stirring until sugar is dissolved. Brush over loaf.
4 Continue to bake 15 minutes longer, or until brown and glazed. Lift to heated serving platter with 2 wide spatulas.

Senegalese Lamb Loaf

Bake at 350° for 1 hour. Makes 8 servings

4 slices bacon, diced
¼ cup sliced green onions
1 pound ground lamb
1 pound ground beef
3 cups cooked rice
¼ cup flaked coconut
¼ cup dried currants
¼ cup chopped peanuts
¼ cup chopped chutney
1 teaspoon salt
1 egg
1 hard-cooked egg, shelled and diced
Chopped parsley
Curry Sauce (recipe follows)

1 Sauté bacon until crisp in a small frying pan; remove with a slotted spoon to a large bowl. Sauté onions in drippings in same pan until soft; combine with bacon.
2 Add lamb and beef to bacon mixture along with rice, coconut, currants, peanuts, chutney, salt, and egg; mix lightly until well-blended. Fold in hard-cooked egg.
3 Spoon mixture into a lightly greased baking pan, 15x10x1; shape into an 8-inch round.
4 Bake in moderate oven (350°) 1 hour, or until crusty-brown.
5 Place loaf on a heated serving platter; sprinkle with parsley. Cut into wedges with a sharp knife. Serve with *Curry Sauce.*

CURRY SAUCE—Chop 1 medium-size onion (½ cup); slice 1 clove of garlic. Sauté both in 2 tablespoons butter or margarine until soft in a small saucepan. Stir in 1 tablespoon curry powder; cook 1 minute. Blend in 1 tablespoon flour and 1 envelope instant chicken broth or 1 teaspoon granulated chicken bouillon; cook, stirring constantly, until bubbly. Stir in 1 jar (about 8 ounces) junior applesauce and 1 cup water; continue cooking and stirring until sauce thickens and boils 1 minute; remove from heat. Stir in 1 tablespoon lemon juice. Makes about 2 cups.

Lamb Stroganoff Pinwheel

Mushroom-noodle stuffing twirls round and round inside each savory slice
Bake at 350° for 1 hour. Makes 6 servings

1 package (8 ounces) fine noodles
2 tablespoons flour
½ cup dairy sour cream
½ cup chopped canned mushrooms
1½ teaspoons salt
2 pounds ground lamb
1 cup soft white bread crumbs
1 egg, slightly beaten
1½ teaspoons instant minced onion
½ cup bottled chili sauce

1 Cook noodles, following label directions; drain. Stir in flour, sour cream, mushrooms, and ½ teaspoon of the salt.
2 Blend lamb with bread crumbs, egg, onion, and remaining 1 teaspoon salt in a large bowl. Pat into a rectangle, 10x12, on foil. Spread 1

cup of the noodle mixture over meat; roll up, jelly-roll fashion. Place, seam side down, in a baking pan. Brush with chili sauce.
3 Bake in moderate oven (350°) 1 hour, or until richly glazed. Reheat remaining noodle mixture to serve with loaf.

Mold Lamb Stroganoff Pinwheel this way

Keep noodle filling in from the edges of meat so it doesn't squeeze out during rolling, then start rolling from a short end. A sheet of foil or wax paper underneath serves as a lifter, and if the meat tends to stick, loosen it with a spatula as you go.

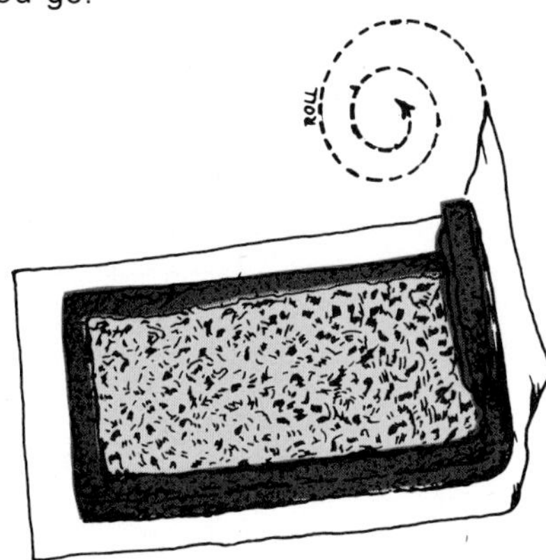

Lamb Stroganoff Pinwheel, pretty enough for a party.

Apple-Glazed Pork Loaf

Bake at 350° for 1½ hours. Makes 8 servings

- *½ cup finely diced celery*
- *1 medium-size onion, chopped (½ cup)*
- *4 tablespoons (½ stick) butter or margarine*
- *1 cup ready-mix corn-bread stuffing*
- *1 tablespoon prepared mustard*
- *½ cup water*
- *1½ pounds ground fresh pork*
- *1 pound ground cooked ham*
- *1 egg*
- *1 cup buttermilk*
- *1 cup apple jelly*
- *2 tablespoons bottled grenadine syrup*

1 Sauté celery and onion in butter or margarine until soft in a large frying pan. Stir in stuffing, mustard, and water; heat, stirring constantly, 1 minute; spoon into a large bowl.
2 Add pork, ham, egg, and buttermilk; mix lightly until well-blended. Press firmly into a baking pan, 9x5x3.
3 Bake in moderate oven (350°) 1 hour; remove from oven, but leave heat on.
4 Pour all juices from pan. Loosen loaf around edges with a knife, then invert into a shallow baking pan.
5 Combine jelly and grenadine syrup in a small saucepan; heat slowly to boiling, then simmer 1 minute. Spoon part over loaf; return to oven.
6 Bake, spooning remaining apple mixture over loaf, 30 minutes, or until richly glazed.
7 Place loaf on a heated serving platter. Garnish with apple slices and watercress, if you wish. Cut loaf into thick slices.

Stuffed Pork Square

Bake at 375° for 50 minutes. Makes 8 servings

- *¼ cup sliced green onions*
- *4 tablespoons (½ stick) butter or margarine*
- *2 cups ready-mix corn-bread stuffing*
- *1 can (12 ounces) whole-kernel corn*
- *1 can (12 ounces) pork luncheon meat*
- *1½ pounds ground pork*
- *⅓ cup quick-cooking rolled oats*
- *1 egg*
- *½ cup milk*
- *1 tablespoon prepared mustard*
- *1 teaspoon salt*
- *¼ teaspoon leaf thyme, crumbled*

1 Sauté onions in butter or margarine until golden in a medium-size frying pan. Stir in stuffing and corn and liquid; remove from heat.
2 Shred luncheon meat with a fork in a large bowl; add ground pork, rolled oats, egg, milk, mustard, salt, and thyme; mix lightly until well-blended.

Chinese Pork Roll, wrapped in a flaky pastry blanket.

3 Line bottom of a baking pan, 8x8x2, with a strip of foil, allowing a 1-inch overhang on two opposite sides. Pat half of the pork mixture into pan; spread with stuffing mixture, then pat remaining pork mixture firmly over top. Invert into a shallow baking pan; peel off foil.
4 Bake in moderate oven (375°) 50 minutes, or until crusty and brown. Cut into serving-size pieces.

●

Chinese Pork Roll

Quick-fix crust bakes richly golden around a jumbo Oriental style loaf
Bake at 350° for 1 hour, then at 375° for 15 minutes. Makes 8 servings

1 medium-size Chinese cabbage (about 2 pounds)
1 large onion, chopped (1 cup)
4 tablespoons (½ stick) butter or margarine
2 pounds ground fresh pork
2 eggs, slightly beaten
¼ cup sifted all-purpose flour
1 can (about 1 pound) mixed Chinese vegetables
2 tablespoons soy sauce
1 package refrigerated crescent dinner rolls
2 tablespoons water

1 Trim cabbage and dice. (There should be about 7 cups.) Combine 1 cup with onion and 2 tablespoons of the butter or margarine in a small frying pan; sauté 5 minutes, or until soft. Blend with pork, eggs, and flour in a large bowl. (Set remaining cabbage and butter or margarine aside for Step 7.)
2 Drain Chinese vegetables well, then pat dry with paper toweling; stir lightly into meat mixture with soy sauce. Pack into a greased loaf pan, 9x5x3.
3 Bake in moderate oven (350°) 1 hour; remove from oven. Raise oven heat to moderate (375°).
4 Unmold loaf into a large shallow baking pan; discard drippings.
5 Remove dinner rolls from package; separate into 4 rectangles. Place over meat loaf, pressing against sides and ends to cover completely.
6 Bake in moderate oven (375°) 15 minutes, or until richly golden.
7 While meat bakes, combine remaining cabbage with remaining 2 tablespoons butter or margarine and water in a large frying pan; cover. Steam 8 minutes, or until cabbage is crisply tender.
8 Spoon cabbage onto a deep serving platter; place meat loaf on top. Cut into thick slices; serve with prepared mustard or bottled duck sauce.

Wrap Chinese Pork Roll like this

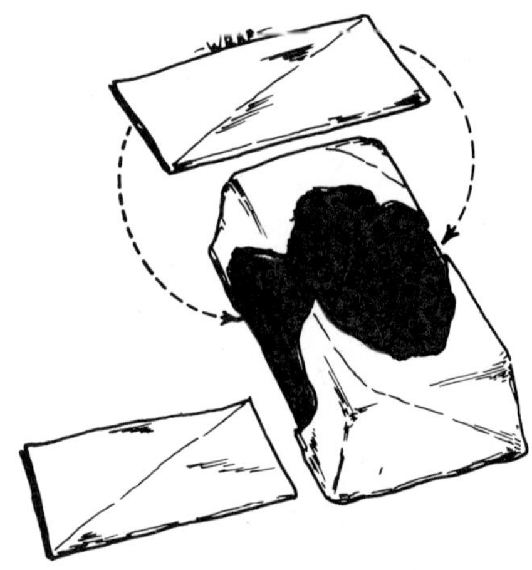

After separating crescent rolls into four rectangles, shape one over each end of loaf to cover completely. Place remaining rectangles across middle and pat down over sides. The middle sections will overlap end pieces slightly, but you can smooth any bumps or ridges with your hands.

●

Glazed Ham Layer Loaf

Bake at 350° for 50 minutes. Makes 8 servings

1½ pounds ground cooked ham
1½ pounds ground veal shoulder
2 cups soft bread crumbs (about 4 slices)

3 eggs
1 medium-size onion, grated
¼ cup prepared mustard
½ teaspoon salt
½ teaspoon ground cloves
½ cup milk
Piquant Fruit Glaze (recipe follows)
Savory Rice Filling (recipe follows)

1 Combine ham, veal, bread crumbs, eggs, onion, mustard, salt, cloves, and milk in large bowl.
2 Pack lightly into 2 eight-inch layer-cake pans; invert onto a large jelly-roll pan; lift off pans.
3 Bake in moderate oven (350°) 30 minutes; brush with *Piquant Fruit Glaze,* bake 20 minutes longer, basting 2 or 3 times, or until done.
4 Place 1 layer, glazed-side down, on platter; cover with *Savory Rice Filling;* top with second layer, glazed-side up; garnish, if desired, with mandarin oranges and parsley.

PIQUANT FRUIT GLAZE—Boil ½ cup brown sugar, firmly packed; ⅓ cup vinegar; ¼ cup canned pineapple juice; and ¼ cup molasses about 10 minutes in saucepan. Makes about 1 cup.

SAVORY RICE FILLING—Cook 1 cup rice, following label directions; stir in 2 tablespoons butter or margarine, then ½ cup finely chopped celery, ¼ cup chopped parsley, and ½ teaspoon grated onion. Makes about 3 cups.

Creamy Mustard Sauce

Fold ½ cup mayonnaise and 4 teaspoons prepared mustard into ½ cup cream, whipped until stiff in a small bowl. Makes 1½ cups.

Ham-Vegetable Loaf

Bake at 350° for 45 minutes. Makes 6 servings

1 large onion, chopped (1 cup)
½ cup chopped celery
½ cup grated, pared raw carrot (about 1 large)
3 tablespoons butter or margarine
1 beef-bouillon cube
½ cup water
1½ pounds ground cooked ham
2 eggs
¼ teaspoon leaf thyme, crumbled
⅛ teaspoon pepper
1 teaspoon lemon juice
MUSTARD SAUCE (recipe follows)

1 Sauté onion, celery, and carrot lightly in butter or margarine in medium-size frying pan; add bouillon cube and water, stirring until cube dissolves; cover; simmer 5 minutes.
2 Combine ground ham, cooked vegetables and liquid, eggs, thyme, pepper, and lemon juice in large bowl; mix lightly just until blended; spoon into a greased loaf pan, 9x5x3.
3 Bake in moderate oven (350°) 45 minutes, or until crisp and golden on top.
4 Loosen around edges and turn out onto heated serving platter; serve with MUSTARD SAUCE.

MUSTARD SAUCE—Combine 1 cup dairy sour cream, 1 tablespoon lemon juice, 2 teaspoons prepared mustard, 1 teaspoon sugar, and ½ teaspoon salt in small bowl; chill to blend flavors. Makes 1 cup.

Currant-Glazed Ham-Loaf

Bake at 350° for 1 hour. Makes 6 servings

Ham-Loaf

1 pound ground fresh pork
1 pound ground cooked ham
1 cup grated raw potato
½ cup grated process cheese
1 small onion, grated
1 egg
1½ teaspoons salt
1 teaspoon Worcestershire sauce
½ teaspoon leaf thyme, crumbled
¼ teaspoon pepper

Glaze

¼ cup currant jelly
1 tablespoon hot water
1 teaspoon prepared mustard

1 Make MEAT LOAF: Combine all ingredients in large bowl; mix lightly with fork; spoon into loaf pan, 9x5x3; invert into shallow pan; carefully remove loaf pan.
2 Make GLAZE: Melt jelly in hot water; add mustard; spread over top of loaf.
3 Bake in moderate oven (350°) 1 hour, or until meat is well done and top is a rich golden brown.

Ham and Cracker Round

Next time you serve ham, cook extra to have on hand for this spicy moist loaf
Bake at 350° for 1 hour. Makes 6 servings

1½ pounds ground cooked ham
1 medium-size onion, peeled
15 unsalted soda crackers
1 egg

¼ *cup water*
½ *teaspoon leaf marjoram, crumbled*
⅛ *teaspoon pepper*
¼ *cup pancake syrup*
1 *teaspoon prepared mustard*
Glazed Peaches (recipe follows)

1 Put ham, onion, and crackers through food chopper, using coarse blade. Mix with egg, water, marjoram, and pepper in medium-size bowl.
2 Shape mixture into a round loaf in greased shallow baking pan; score top in crisscross pattern with knife.
3 Bake in moderate oven (350°) 30 minutes; baste with mixture of pancake syrup and prepared mustard. Bake 30 minutes longer, or until richly browned. Serve in wedges with *Glazed Peaches.*
GLAZED PEACHES—Arrange 1 can (about 1 pound) drained cling peach halves, cut side up, in pie plate. Dot with 2 tablespoons butter or margarine; sprinkle with 2 tablespoons brown sugar mixed with ¼ teaspoon ground ginger. Bake in moderate oven (350°), basting once with buttery syrup in dish, 20 minutes, or until richly glazed. Makes 6 servings.

Upside-Down Ham Square

Baked ham left over? Use six cups of ground meat to replace the canned variety
Bake at 350° for 1 hour. Makes 8 servings

1 *can (1 pound) whole sweet potatoes*
¼ *cup firmly packed brown sugar*
1 *tablespoon butter or margarine, melted*
½ *teaspoon salt*
¾ *teaspoon pumpkin-pie spice*
1 *two-pound canned ham*
2 *medium-size apples*
1 *medium-size onion, peeled and quartered*
1 *cup soft rye-bread crumbs*
2 *eggs, slightly beaten*
¼ *cup apple juice*
¼ *teaspoon pepper*

1 Line a baking pan, 8x8x2, with a double-thick piece of foil long enough to fit across bottom and up sides of pan with a 1-inch overhang; lightly grease foil.
2 Mash sweet potatoes with a fork in a medium-size bowl; beat in brown sugar, melted butter or margarine, salt, and pumpkin-pie spice. Spread in an even layer in foil-lined pan.

3 Scrape gelatin coating from ham, then cut ham into small chunks. Pare apples, quarter, and core. Put ham, apples, and onion through a food chopper, using a coarse blade; place in a large bowl. Stir in bread crumbs, eggs, apple juice, and pepper. Pack lightly in an even layer over potato mixture in pan.
4 Bake in moderate oven (350°) 1 hour, or until firm and lightly golden.
5 Cool in pan or on a wire rack 5 minutes; invert onto a serving platter; peel off foil. Garnish loaf with thin slices of unpared apple, if you wish.

Follow these tips when making Upside-Down Ham Square

For trim unmolding, line your baking pan first with a sheet of foil, letting it extend over the sides about an inch. Then add the sweet-potato and meat layers. After baking, pull up on foil to loosen loaf, cover pan with plate, and flip both over at the same time.

TWO LOW-CALORIE MEAT LOAVES

Veal "Mock Chicken" Loaf

Bake at 325° for 1 hour. Makes 6 servings at 234 calories each

1½ *pounds ground veal*
1 *egg, beaten*
1 *onion, chopped fine*
2 *envelopes or teaspoons instant chicken broth*
3 *tablespoons dried parsley flakes*
1 *cup minced celery*

Tall and tempting: Beef Ring piled high with Candied Carrots. Garlic, onion and catsup give the loaf zip.

1 teaspoon poultry seasoning
¼ teaspoon pepper

Mix all ingredients lightly and shape into a loaf. Place on a rack in a baking pan, bake in moderate oven (325°) for 1 hour. Serve with *Low-Calorie Cranberry Sauce* and *Low-Calorie Chicken Gravy (recipes follow).*

LOW-CALORIE CRANBERRY SAUCE—Add 2 cups water and ½ cup sugar to one pound cranberries. Simmer, uncovered, until skins pop. Remove from heat and stir in no-calorie sweetener to equal 1½ cups sugar. Makes 4 cups—9 calories per tablespoon, half the calories of regular cranberry sauce.

LOW-CALORIE CHICKEN GRAVY—Add 1½ tablespoons flour, 2 envelopes or teaspoons instant chicken broth and 1 teaspoon parsley flakes to 1½ cups cold water. Heat slowly in a saucepan, stirring constantly. Simmer until thickened. Makes 10 calories per serving.

Beef Ring with Candied Carrots

Bake at 325° for 1 hour. Makes 6 servings at 279 calories each

1½ pounds lean ground beef
1 egg, beaten
3 tablespoons water
4 tablespoons catsup
3 tablespoons grated onion
1 teaspoon salt
½ teaspoon pepper
Dash of garlic powder
1 tablespoon bread crumbs

1 Combine all ingredients except bread crumbs. Mix lightly; add only enough water to make mixiture workable. Pat gently into a 6-cup ring mold, then invert on a rack in a baking pan. Remove ring mold. Or: Shape meat loaf by hand into a big "doughnut."
2 Sprinkle top with crumbs, then bake in moderate oven (325°) for 1 hour. Remove to a platter and fill center with candied carrots.

EASY SUGARLESS "CANDIED" CARROTS—Heat the contents of a 1-pound can of carrots in a saucepan and bring to boiling; drain. Add three tablespoons diet maple syrup, one tablespoon lemon juice, one teaspoon parsley flakes, one teaspoon butter or margarine, salt and pepper. Simmer until most of the liquid evaporates and the carrots are nicely glazed.

TIPS FOR CALORIE-WISE MEAT-LOAF MAKERS

- Garlic, mustard, Worcestershire, horseradish, chili, catsup, herbs, spices and seasonings—most of the real flavor-makers are low in calories. Bread crumbs, rice and other starchy stuffers add little flavor and lots of empty calories.
- The better-choice meat-stretchers are tomatoes, onions, green peppers, mushrooms, celery and such. But why stop there? Grated carrots, drained bean sprouts, chopped string beans, cubed eggplant . . . almost any vegetable you like can agreeably fill out a meat loaf with flavor, texture and added vitamins.
- Meat loaf is best baked on top of a rack in a baking pan—not *in* a loaf pan or other container that traps melting fat. Every tablespoon that drains away is worth 125 calories.

THREE WAYS TO SHAPE INDIVIDUAL MINI LOAVES

Pat meat mixture into muffin pan cups; brush each generously with barbecue sauce.

Divide meat mixture in portions; shape each into a log; top with catsup.

Mold meat mixture in a custard cup, then turn out into a shallow baking pan.

WAYS TO SHAPE MEAT LOAVES

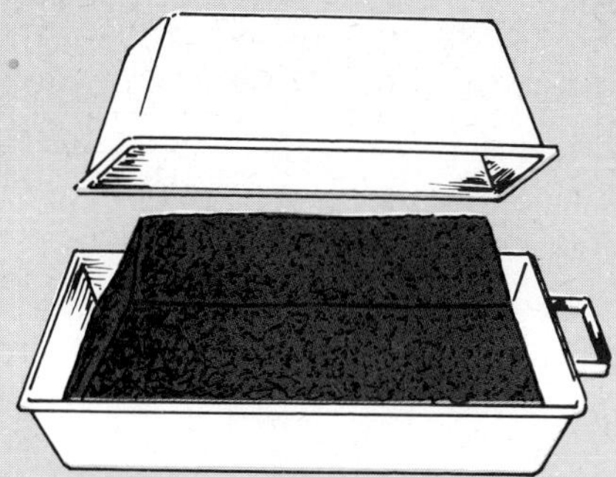

Most-Popular Loaf
A jiffy—that's all this shaping trick takes. Press meat into a bread pan, then invert into a shallow pan for baking. Want to go simpler still? Bake the loaf right in the bread pan.

Casserole Easy
A shallow baking dish—round, square, or oblong—makes an ideal mold for meat loaf, and most are attractive enough to carry right to the table for serving. For a subtle flavor touch, top loaf with a bay leaf before baking.

Bowl-'em-over Round
Here's another molding trick with a casserole, or you can use a regular mixing bowl. Place the meat in the bowl and turn it upside down into a pan; lift off bowl. Serving tip: Divide the loaf into quarters and slice each quarter.

Easy-as-pie Whirligig
A pie plate is the baker for this inviting loaf. After pressing meat into the plate, mark it into wedges and outline each with a ribbon of catsup. Cut between marks after baking; lift out each sauce-topped wedge with a spatula.

SEVEN

BURGERS

FOUR EASY STEPS TO PERFECT HAMBURGERS

Follow a tip your supermarket uses and handle ground meat as little as possible, for the gentler your touch, the jucier and tenderer the burger.

Season each 1 pound of ground beef with 1 teaspoon salt and ⅛ teaspoon pepper. Nothing more is really needed, but for variety, you may want to add other seasonings, as many of our recipes suggest.

Use a mixing fork to blend in seasonings. Even an egg will mix in quickly without beating first.

Making four or six patties? Pat out seasoned meat about 1 inch thick, cut into even mounds, and shape lightly with your hands. For small appetites, or for children, you may prefer to divide each mound again, then shape it into a thinner patty.

HOW TO COOK BURGERS JUST RIGHT

To pan-fry: Heat a heavy frying pan until sizzling hot. (A few drops of water sprinkled into the pan should dance about.) For plain burgers, there's no need to add any fat, but you can sprinkle the pan lightly with salt, if you wish, to prevent sticking. For burgers seasoned with extras such as egg, bread crumbs, or rolled oats, you may need to add a little butter or margarine or salad oil. Lay patties in hot pan and lower heat to medium. Cook 1-inch-thick patties 8 minutes on each side for medium. For ½-inch-thick patties, allow 4 minutes on each side for medium.

To broil: Remove broiler pan, then turn heat to BROIL. Lay patties, without touching, on rack in pan, then slide back into broiler about 4 inches from heat. Broil 1-inch-thick patties 6 minutes on each side for medium. Since thin patties—those ½ inch thick—will cook through before they brown on the outside, it is better, if your choice is medium-rare, to pan-fry them.

Turn the meat just once, for flipping it over and over tends to dry it. Juices oozing out around edges are your clue for turning.

Undercook a hamburger if it has to stand. Each patty has enough heat in it to continue some cooking, and you can reheat it without overcooking.

A hit at every picnic: plump charcoal-grilled burgers.

IF PATTIES HAVE BEEN FROZEN

Cooking patties while frozen is all right, but it takes slightly longer and the meat is likely to turn out well-done. We prefer to thaw the meat first this way: Remove patties from the freezer a day ahead and store in their sealed wrapper in the refrigerator. If time is short and you must cook them frozen, follow these tips:

To pan-fry: Brown each side quickly in a hot frying pan, then lower heat and cook, turning two or three times, until meat is done as you like it.

To broil: Set the broiler pan farther from the heat than when cooking fresh patties and turn several times.

WAYS TO VARY THE SHAPE OF HAMBURGERS

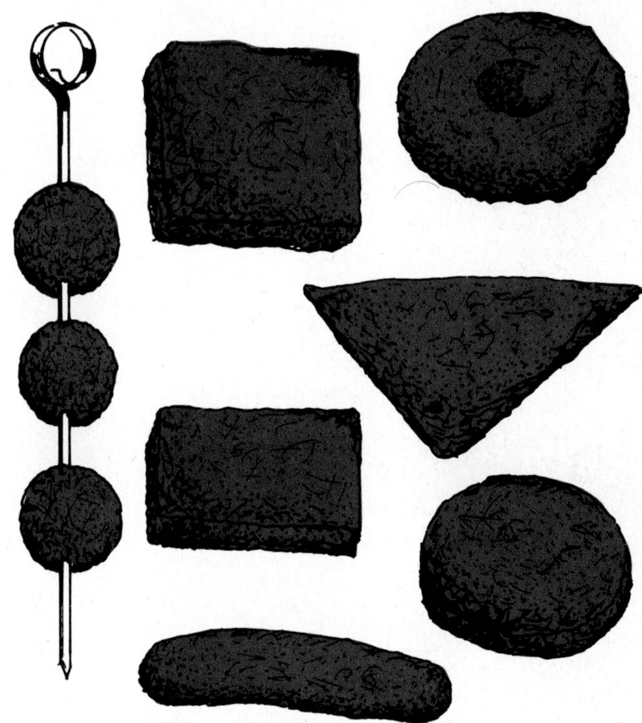

Hamburgers take to so many stylings, and it's fun to make rounds, squares, logs, rectangles, or triangles to fit different shapes of breads, buns, and rolls. "Doughnut" patty even has a custom-made center to hold catsup or mustard. Tiny balls molded around an olive and strung on a skewer are best skillet-grilled, for meat is soft.

QUICK AND EASY FLAVOR TRICKS FOR HAMBURGERS

"Guess What" Grilled Burgers

Makes 8 servings

2 pounds ground beef
2 teaspoons salt
¼ teaspoon freshly ground pepper

Mix ground beef lightly with salt and pepper. Stir in 1 medium-size onion, grated, if you wish. Shape any of these ways, stacking each two patties with waxed paper or foil between:

Sixteen thin rounds to fit hamburger buns, round bread slices, or large baking powder biscuits.
Sixteen rectangles to fit frankfurter rolls, club rolls, or 3-inch pieces of French bread.
Sixteen squares to fit sliced sandwich bread.

Put each two patties together with any of these fillings:

Thinly sliced tomatoes sprinkled lightly with seasoned salt and grated Parmesan cheese.

Canned baked beans seasoned with crumbled crisp bacon and a dash of catsup.
Chili con carne spooned right from the can.
Canned French fried onions, coarsely crushed.
Drained canned chopped or sliced mushrooms.
Dill, sweet, or crisp cucumber pickle slices.
Assorted sliced cheeses: American, Swiss, pimiento, sharp Cheddar.
Crumbled or mashed blue cheese mixed with an equal amount of cream cheese.
Grated Parmesan cheese or sharp cheese spread plain or mixed with a little chili sauce.
Thinly sliced frankfurters topped with mustard.
Pickle relish blended with chopped celery, grated carrot, and a little mayonnaise or salad dressing.

Grill this way: Press edges of filled patties together to seal. Grill over hot coals until meat is done as you like it. Put together, sandwich style, with your choice of buns or bread.

More-and-More Burgers

Makes 4 servings

1 pound ground beef
1 teaspoon salt
⅛ teaspoon pepper

Mix ground beef lightly with salt and pepper, then mix in one of these special seasoners before shaping patties:

½ cup bottled barbecue sauce.
1 or 2 green onions, sliced thin.
1 can (2¼ or 3 ounces) deviled ham, 1 teaspoon prepared mustard, and 1 tablespoon pickle relish.
½ cup grated Cheddar cheese and ¼ cup catsup.
⅓ cup chopped walnuts, peanuts, or toasted almonds.
¼ cup dairy sour cream, 1 tablespoon chopped parsley, and a generous dash of thyme and oregano.
½ cup chopped fresh mushrooms or drained canned ones.
¼ cup chopped stuffed green olives or 2 tablespoons each chopped pimiento and ripe olives.
½ cup grated pared carrot, 2 tablespoons grated radishes, and 1 teaspoon grated onion.
¼ cup grated Parmesan cheese, ¼ cup canned tomato sauce, and ¼ teaspoon oregano.
½ cup cooked rice, 2 teaspoons soy sauce, and 1 sliced green onion.
3 slices crumbled crisp bacon and ½ cup canned applesauce.
½ cup crushed cheese crackers or other flavored crackers, or plain or seasoned potato chips or corn chips.

Shape into patties. Grill over hot coals until meat is done as you like it. Put together, sandwich style, with your choice of buns or bread.

Toppers for Plain Burgers

Makes enough for 4 to 6 sandwiches

Make plain burgers and grill over hot coals until meat is done as you like it, then top with any of these seasoning extras:

1 tablespoon butter or margarine heated with ¼ cup chili sauce and ¼ teaspoon chili powder just until bubbly.

½ package (3 or 4 ounces) pimiento, relish, or chives cream cheese blended with ¼ cup dairy sour cream.

1 tablespoon each melted butter or margarine and bottled garlic-flavor French dressing mixed with 1 teaspoon chopped parsley and ½ teaspoon cut chives.

1 tablespoon flour blended with 1 tablespoon butter or margarine, ¼ teaspoon curry powder, ¼ teaspoon salt, and 1 can (3 or 4 ounces) chopped mushrooms and liquid, and cooked until sauce thickens and boils 1 minute.

½ can French fried onions heated with ¼ cup catsup just until bubbly.

2 tablespoons butter or margarine heated with ¼ cup catsup and 1 tablespoon bottled steak sauce.

2 cups shredded cabbage seasoned with bottled coleslaw dressing and a few sliced stuffed green olives and bits of crisp bacon.

½ can (1 pound) barbecue beans or baked beans heated with ½ cup grated Cheddar cheese.

Instant mashed potatoes blended with 1 or 2 sliced green onions.

Cooksaver Tip:

Hot cooked burgers taste twice as good topped with frosty butter drops to melt in 'way down deep. To fix them, choose any of the buttery spreads listed. Drop, a teaspoonful at a time, into a tiny mound in a foil- or wax-paper-lined ice-cube tray; chill until firm. At cookout time, pile them into a bowl half-filled with ice, ready to put on burgers.

Buttery Spreads for Buns and Breads

Makes enough for 4 to 6 sandwiches

Start with 4 tablespoons (½ stick) softened butter or margarine and blend in any of these seasoners, then spread on buns, rolls, or bread:

½ crushed clove garlic and 1 tablespoon grated Parmesan cheese.

1 tablespoon chopped parsley and 1 teaspoon finely cut chives.

1 can (2¼ ounces) deviled ham and ½ teaspoon prepared horseradish-mustard.

1 tablespoon hamburger or hot-dog relish.

1 teaspoon bottled steak sauce and ½ teaspoon chili powder.

1 tablespoon chopped stuffed green olives or chopped ripe olives.

2 tablespoons crumbled blue cheese and ½ teaspoon Worcestershire sauce.

¼ cup mashed peeled avocado, 1 tablespoon chili sauce, and ¼ teaspoon onion salt.

¼ teaspoon curry powder and 2 tablespoons catsup or chili sauce.

1 small onion, minced, and ¼ cup chili sauce.

1 tablespoon mayonnaise or salad dressing, 1 tablespoon chopped dill pickle, and ¼ teaspoon garlic salt.

¼ cup grated Cheddar cheese and 2 tablespoons pickle relish.

2 tablespoons grated Parmesan cheese and a dash of oregano.

¼ cup smoky-cheese spread (from a 5-ounce jar) and ½ teaspoon prepared mustard.

1 tablespoon catsup, 1 teaspoon lemon juice, ½ teaspoon prepared mustard, and ¼ teaspoon chili powder.

1 tablespoon finely chopped walnuts, peanuts, or almonds and ½ teaspoon seasoned salt.

Just-Plain-Good Burgers

Makes 4 servings

1 pound ground beef
1 small onion, grated
1 teaspoon salt
⅛ teaspoon pepper
4 split hamburger buns, buttered and toasted

1 Mix ground beef lightly with seasonings; shape into 4 patties about 1 inch thick.
2 Pan-fry over medium heat 8 minutes on each side for medium, or broil, 4 inches from heat, 6 minutes on each side for medium, or until meat is done as you like it.
3 Put together, sandwich style, with toasted buns.

Variations:

TIVOLI BURGERS—Prepare mixture for *Just-Plain-Good Burgers,* broil, following directions above. Mix ¼ cup mashed blue cheese, 1 tablespoon mayonnaise or salad dressing, and ½ teaspoon soy sauce; spread on patties. Return to broiler until cheese is bubbly. Serve, sandwich style, in toasted buns.

HERBED BURGERS—Prepare mixture for *Just-Plain-Good Burgers,* adding ½ teaspoon mixed salad herbs. Pan-fry or broil, following directions above. Cream 1 tablespoon butter or margarine with 1 teaspoon finely cut chives; spread over hot patties. Serve, sandwich style, in toasted buns.

CHILI-CHEESE BURGERS—Prepare mixture for *Just-Plain-Good Burgers,* adding ½ cup diced Muenster cheese and ½ teaspoon chili powder. Pan-fry or broil, following directions above. Serve, sandwich style, in toasted buns.

All-American Cheeseburgers

Makes 4 servings

1 pound ground beef
1 teaspoon salt
⅛ teaspoon pepper
2 teaspoons catsup
8 slices (half an 8-ounce package) process sharp American cheese
8 slices tomato
8 slices Bermuda onion
4 slices green pepper
4 slices crisp cooked bacon
4 split hamburger buns, toasted and buttered

1 Mix ground beef lightly with salt and pepper; shape into 4 patties about 1-inch thick.
2 Pan-fry over medium heat 8 minutes on each side for medium, or until meat is done as you like it. Brush tops lightly with catsup; cover each burger with a cheese slice. (Heat from meat will melt cheese).
3 Top each with a tomato and onion slice; put together, sandwich style, on buttered buns which have first been topped with one slice each of green pepper, onion, tomato and cheese. Top each cheeseburger with a crisp slice of bacon.

The Family Circle Big Burger

Makes 6 servings

½ cup mayonnaise or salad dressing
¼ cup chili sauce
¼ cup chopped green pepper
1 teaspoon instant minced onion
2 pounds ground round
2 teaspoons salt
¼ teaspoon pepper
2 tablespoons butter or margarine
6 slices process American cheese (from an 8-ounce package)
1 large dill pickle, cut into 12 slices
6 thin tomato slices
1 small onion, peeled, sliced thinly and separated into rings

American Classic: hamburger on a bun.

The superburger: *begin with a bun, build up layers of cucumber, onion, tomato, cheese and fat juicy burger.*

1½ cups finely shredded lettuce (¼ small head)
9 split hamburger buns, or 6 high hamburger buns or soft buns, split into thirds, toasted

1 Combine mayonnaise or salad dressing, chili sauce, green pepper, and instant minced onion in a small bowl; mix well. Reserve for step 6.
2 Mix ground round lightly with salt and pepper. Shape into 12 thin patties.
3 Pan-fry 6 burgers in part of butter or margarine over medium heat in a large skillet 3 minutes on each side for rare, or until meat is done as you like it.
4 Place a slice of cheese on each of the burgers and broil, 4 inches from heat, about 2 minutes, or just until cheese melts slightly. Pan-fry the remaining hamburgers in remaining butter or margarine in same skillet.
5 To assemble: Place the cheeseburgers on the bottom halves of 6 hamburger buns; top each with 2 dill-pickle slices. Place split buns on the top, sandwich fashion.
6 Top buns with remaining hamburgers, then tomato and onion slices, and ¼ cup shredded lettuce. Spread 2 tablespoons of the prepared sauce on the cut top portion of the buns. Place over the lettuce. Secure with a toothpick or wooden skewer, if you wish.

Party trick: hotdog-shaped hamburgers, lacy onion rings.

Crunchy Cheeseburgers
Makes 6 servings

1 pound ground beef
½ cup wheat-flakes cereal
1 cup grated sharp Cheddar cheese (4 ounces)
½ cup chopped walnuts
½ teaspoon seasoned salt
½ cup water
12 slices rye bread, toasted and buttered

1 Mix ground beef lightly with wheat-flakes cereal, cheese, walnuts, seasoned salt, and water; shape into 6 patties about ½-inch thick.
2 Broil, 3 inches from heat, 4 minutes on each side for medium, or until meat is done as you like it. Put together, sandwich style, with toasted bread.

Hamburger Clubs
Makes 6 servings

2 pounds ground beef
2 teaspoons bottled steak sauce
2 packages (9 ounces each) frozen cut green beans
1 can (10½ ounces) condensed cream of mushroom soup
12 slices bacon (about ½ pound)
6 split hamburger buns, buttered
3 slices mozzarella or pizza cheese, cut into 12 strips
1 can (about 3 ounces) French-fried onion rings

1 Mix ground beef lightly with steak sauce; shape into 6 patties about 1 inch thick.
2 Cook green beans, following label directions; drain. Stir in soup; heat, stirring carefully so as not to break beans, just until bubbly.
3 While beans cook, place meat patties on one side of rack in broiler pan and bacon on the other. Broil, 4 inches from heat and without turning bacon, 5 minutes, or just until bacon starts to crisp; remove. Continue broiling patties 1 minute; turn; broil 5 minutes longer for medium, or until meat is done as you like it.
4 Place each patty on a buttered bun half; arrange cheese strips over each to form an X. Spoon hot green-bean mixture onto remaining bun halves, dividing evenly; crisscross bacon, uncrisped side up, over top.
5 Broil 1 minute longer, or just until cheese melts and bacon is crisp. Garnish meat patties with French-fried onion rings. (To crisp, heat in shallow pan in oven.)

Sweet-Sour Pagoda Burgers
Meat patties are stacked three high with pineapple and sliced vegetables, then served with rice and a zippy sauce.
Makes 4 servings

1½ pounds ground beef
1 can (5 ounces) water chestnuts, drained and chopped fine
1 egg, beaten
4 teaspoons soy sauce (for meat)
1 can (about 9 ounces) sliced pineapple, drained
1 large tomato, cut in 4 slices
5 tablespoons butter or margarine
Salt and pepper
1 tablespoon cornstarch
1 tablespoon molasses
2 tablespoons soy sauce (for sauce)
1 cup water
1 tablespoon lemon juice
½ cup sliced green onions
3 cups cooked hot rice (¾ cup uncooked)
4 slices cucumber

Hamburger Clubs with green beans and melty mozzarella.

1 Combine ground beef, chopped water chestnuts, egg, and 4 teaspoons soy sauce in a large bowl; mix lightly with a fork. Divide mixture in half.
2 Shape half into 4 patties about ½ inch thick. Shape two thirds of remaining, then other third, into 4 medium-size and 4 small patties. (Keep all 12 patties evenly thick so they will cook in the same time.) Place, close together, on rack in broiler pan.
3 Broil, following range manufacturer's directions, 4 minutes; turn. Place pineapple and tomato slices beside meat; dot with 3 tablespoons of the butter or margarine; sprinkle tomatoes with salt and pepper. Broil 4 minutes longer for medium, or until meat is done as you like it.
4 Blend cornstarch, molasses, and the 2 tablespoons soy sauce in a small saucepan; add water. Cook, stirring constantly, until sauce thickens and boils 3 minutes. Stir in remaining 2 tablespoons butter or margarine, lemon juice, and green onions.
5 When ready to serve, spoon rice onto 4 serving plates; place a pineapple slice on each; top each with a large meat patty, tomato slice, medium-size patty, cucumber slice, and small meat patty. Spoon some of the sauce over each, then serve remaining separately. Garnish each with a kumquat "flower," if you wish.
Note— To fix kumquat "flower," make 4 lengthwise cuts in a preserved kumquat from tip almost to stem end; place a tiny sweet pickle in center; thread onto a wooden pick and stick into meat patties.

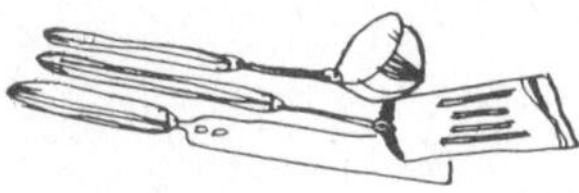

Pot o' Gold Burgers

For a husky open-face sandwich with a difference, crown each meat patty with a sunny fried egg.
Makes 4 servings

1½ pounds ground beef
1 teaspoon seasoned salt
1 tablespoon Worcestershire sauce
4 slices Bermuda onion
4 tablespoons (½ stick) butter or margarine
4 eggs
1 large tomato, cut in 4 slices
2 split hamburger buns, buttered and toasted

1 Season ground beef with seasoned salt and Worcestershire sauce; shape lightly into 4 patties about 1 inch thick.
2 Sauté onion slices, turning once, in 2 tablespoons of the butter or margarine in a large frying pan, 4 minutes, or just until lightly golden. Remove and keep warm for Step 5. (Set remaining butter or margarine aside for cooking eggs in Step 4.)
3 Pan-fry meat patties, turning once, in same frying pan 16 minutes for medium, or until meat is done as you like it.
4 While meat cooks, melt remaining 2 tablespoons butter or margarine in a medium-size frying pan; break eggs into pan; cover. Cook slowly 3 to 4 minutes, or just until yolks set.
5 When ready to serve, place a tomato slice on each bun half; top with an onion slice, meat patty, and a fried egg. (Cut around whites of eggs to separate neatly.) Garnish with carrot and celery sticks, if you wish.

Pacifica Patio Burgers

Makes 4 servings

1½ pounds ground beef or lamb
1 small onion, grated
2 teaspoons Worcestershire sauce
1 teaspoon salt
¼ teaspoon pepper
3 slices process Swiss cheese, cut into thin strips
4 split hamburger buns, toasted and buttered
Lettuce
4 thick slices tomato
Mayonnaise or salad dressing
Onion rings
Red-pepper relish

1 Mix ground beef lightly with onion, Worcestershire sauce, salt, and pepper; shape into 4 patties about 1 inch thick.
2 Grill over hot coals until meat is almost as done as you like it. Crisscross cheese strips on top; dividing evenly; grill 1 minute longer, or until cheese melts.
3 Cover bottom halves of buns with lettuce. Spread tomato slices with mayonnaise or salad dressing; place on top of lettuce, then top with a broiled meat patty. Garnish with a few onion rings and a generous spoonful of red-pepper relish. Serve with remaining bun halves.

Bonus Burgers

Each burger has a generous six ounces of meat plus a zippy topping
Makes 4 servings

1 small onion, chopped (¼ cup)
1 tablespoon vegetable oil

- *¼ cup ready-mix bread stuffing*
- *3 tablespoons water*
- *1½ pounds beef*
- *1 tablespoon bottled steak sauce*
- *1 teaspoon salt*
- *1 tablespoon crumbled blue cheese*

1 Sauté onion lightly in vegetable oil in small frying pan; stir in bread stuffing and water; remove from heat; save for Step 3.

2 Combine ground beef, steak sauce, and salt in medium-size bowl; form lightly into 4 patties; make a slight depression in top of each to hold stuffing.

3 Broil, top side down, with meat 5 to 6 inches from heat, about 6 minutes; turn; fill centers with stuffing mixture; top with crumbled blue cheese; broil about 6 minutes * longer, or until done as you like them.

* If meat has to be broiled closer than 5 to 6 inches from heat, add stuffing and crumbled-blue-cheese topping about 3 minutes before meat is done (stuffing may burn if cooked too close to broiler heat).

Pacifica Patio Burgers are lamb burgers crowned with Swiss cheese.

BURGER BONANZA

Hamburgers Diane
Makes 6 servings

2 pounds ground round
2 teaspoons seasoned salt
2 teaspoons seasoned pepper
4 tablespoons (½ stick) butter or margarine
2 tablespoons vegetable oil
2 tablespoons prepared mustard
2 tablespoons lemon juice
1 tablespoon Worcestershire sauce
¼ cup chopped parsley
Pimiento
Parsley sprigs

1 Lightly mix ground round, seasoned salt, and

seasoned pepper in a large bowl. Gently shape into 6 large hamburgers, 1 inch thick.

2 Melt 2 tablespoons of the butter or margarine in a large heavy skillet; remove from heat; blend in oil and mustard; return to heat.

3 Sauté hamburgers over medium heat 4 minutes on each side (for rare); remove and keep warm.

4 Stir lemon juice, Worcestershire sauce, and remaining 2 tablespoons butter or margarine into skillet; stir over low heat until well-blended with drippings; stir in chopped parsley; spoon over steaks. Garnish with pimiento and parsley sprigs. Hamburgers may be served on toasted slices of French bread and accompanied by buttered green beans, if you wish.

How to pare the price of a classic: sauté hamburgers à la Diane instead of steak. They're easy and elegant.

Heavenly Hamburgers on Savory Cheese Dreams

Makes 6 servings

1½ pounds ground beef
1½ teaspoons salt
⅛ teaspoon pepper
6 tomato slices
3 slices bacon, halved
6 slices French bread
6 slices process American cheese, halved diagonally
Leaf oregano, crumbled

1 Combine ground beef, salt, and pepper in medium-size bowl; shape lightly into 6 oval patties; place on broiler rack.
2 Broil, with top of patties 4 inches from heat, 5 to 7 minutes; turn; broil about 3 minutes.
3 Top each with a tomato slice and bacon strip; broil 1 to 2 minutes.
4 Place bread slices on broiler rack with patties; toast; turn; top each with 2 cheese triangles; sprinkle with oregano.
5 Toast about 3 minutes, or until cheese bubbles and browns.
6 Serve a hamburger on top of each cheese dream.

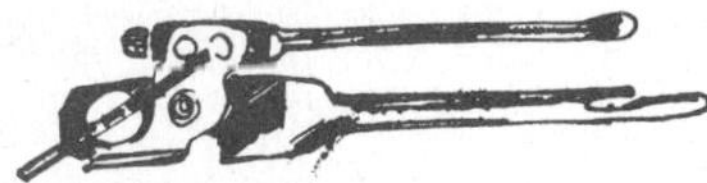

Burger-Tomato Towers

Makes 6 servings

2 pounds ground beef
1 teaspoon seasoned salt
2 large tomatoes
1 can (3 or 4 ounces) mushroom caps
3 tablespoons butter or margarine
3 split hamburger buns, toasted

1 Mix ground beef lightly with seasoned salt; shape into 6 patties about 1 inch thick.
2 Pan-fry over medium heat 8 minutes on each side for medium, or until meat is done as you like it.
3 While meat cooks, remove stem ends from tomatoes; cut each tomato crosswise into 3 thick slices. Drain mushrooms, saving liquid for next step. Sauté tomato slices and mushroom caps in butter or margarine in a second large frying pan, turning tomatoes once, just until heated through.
4 Place a meat patty on each bun half on a heated serving platter. Heat liquid from mushrooms in same frying pan; spoon over patties. Top each with a tomato slice; garnish with mushroom caps and parsley, if you wish.

Hamburger Foldovers

Makes 8 servings

2 pounds ground beef
1½ teaspoons salt
¼ teaspoon pepper
1 package (4 ounces) shredded Cheddar cheese
¼ cup bottled steak sauce
8 split hamburger buns
2 medium-size tomatoes, sliced
1 large onion, peeled, sliced, and separated in rings

1 Mix ground beef lightly with salt and pepper; divide into 8 portions.
2 Pat each into a 6-inch round on a piece of wax paper or foil; spoon about 2 tablespoons cheese in center. Fold round in half, using paper or foil to lift meat; press edges together to seal. Brush patties with steak sauce.
3 Grill over hot coals, turning and brushing with more steak sauce, until meat is done as you like it.
4 Toast buns on grill, then butter, if you wish. Put together, sandwich style, with meat patties, tomato slices, and onion rings.

Cooksaver Tip:
Big thin hamburger patties or squares are easy to fold in half moons or triangles if patted out first on foil or waxed paper to use as a "lifter."

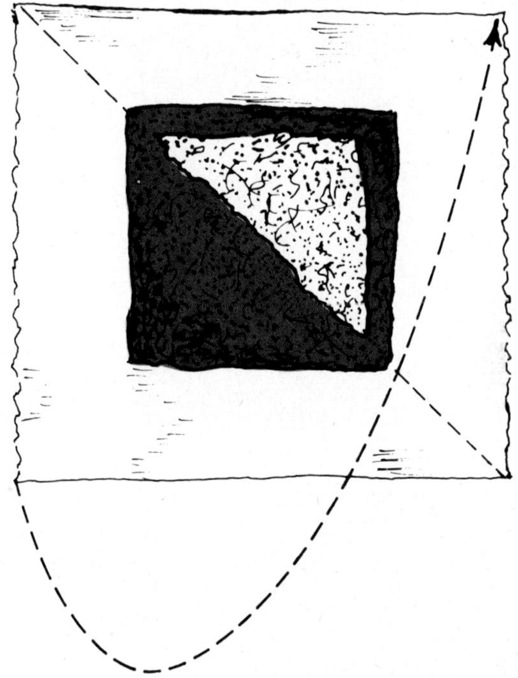

What an entrance Burger-Tomato Towers make at a party. No one will suspect they're such a snap to prepare.

Cheeseburger Dagwoods
Makes 4 servings

1 pound ground beef
1 teaspoon salt
⅛ teaspoon pepper
4 slices process American cheese (from an 8-ounce package)
4 slices of bread, buttered
Prepared sandwich spread
4 cherry tomatoes
4 stuffed green olives

1 Season ground beef with salt and pepper and shape into 4 square patties, just the size of a slice of bread.

Make them round, make them square—no matter what shape, hamburgers and cheeseburgers are tops.

2 Pan-fry, turning once, in a large frying pan, 8 minutes for medium, or until meat is done as you like it. Place cheese slices over top; cover pan; turn off heat and let stand 1 minute to melt cheese.
3 Spread bread with sandwich spread. Place cheeseburgers on bread and garnish with cherry tomatoes and stuffed olives, skewered on decorative wooden toothpicks.

●

Burgers Kun Koki
Makes 8 servings

¼ cup vegetable oil
¼ cup soy sauce
2 tablespoons corn syrup
1 tablespoon lemon juice
½ teaspoon ground ginger
¼ teaspoon garlic powder
2 green onions, sliced thin
2 pounds ground beef
8 split hamburger buns, buttered

1 Mix vegetable oil, soy sauce, corn syrup, lemon juice, ginger, garlic powder, and green onions in a large shallow pan.
2 Shape ground beef into 8 patties about ¾ inch thick. Dip in sauce mixture to coat both sides, then place in a single layer in same pan. Chill 3 to 4 hours to season.
3 When ready to cook, remove patties from sauce and grill over hot coals, brushing several times with the remaining sauce, until meat is done as you like it.
4 Toast buns on grill, if you wish; put together, sandwich style, with meat patties.

The makings of a great beach party: Burgers Kun Koki (on the grill), Skillet Enchiladas and Slumgullion.

Deviled Steaks and Onions
Makes 6 servings

6 large onions, peeled and sliced
4 tablespoons (½ stick) butter or margarine
1 teaspoon salt
¼ cup water
2 pounds ground beef
2 tablespoons prepared mustard
2 tablespoons vegetable oil
2 tablespoons Worcestershire sauce

1 Combine onions, butter or margarine, salt, and water in a large frying pan.
2 Heat, stirring several times, to boiling; cover. Steam 10 minutes, or until soft; uncover. Cook, stirring often, 15 minutes longer, or until liquid has evaporated and onions are golden.
3 While onions cook, shape ground beef lightly into 6 oval patties, about ¾ inch thick. Place on rack in broiler pan.
4 Combine mustard, vegetable oil, and Worcestershire sauce in a small bowl; brush about half over patties.
5 Broil, 4 to 5 inches from heat, 5 minutes; turn. Brush tops with remaining mustard mixture. Broil 5 minutes longer for medium, or until beef is as done as you like it.
6 Place patties on heated serving plates; spoon onions on top.

●

Golden Gate Saucy Burgers
Makes 12 servings

3 pounds ground beef
1 large onion, grated
1 egg

With Golden Gate Saucy Burgers, picnickers get their choice of toppings— from nut to chili to tomato-sauced spaghetti to a rich golden rarebit.

1 *cup canned applesauce*
2 *teaspoons salt*
¼ *teaspoon pepper*
12 *split hamburger buns, toasted and buttered*
Chili Topping (recipe follows)
Salty-nut Topping (recipe follows)
Rarebit Topping (recipe follows)
Spaghetti Topping (recipe follows)

1 Mix ground beef lightly with onion, egg, applesauce, and seasonings until well-blended; shape into 12 patties about 1 inch thick.
2 Grill 8 minutes on each side for medium, or over hot coals, or until meat is done as you like it.
3 Place each patty on half a roll; spoon a topping of your choice over; put together with remaining halves of rolls.

Chili Topping
Makes about 4 cups

1 *medium-size onion, chopped (½ cup)*
2 *teaspoons chili powder*
2 *tablespoons olive oil or vegetable oil*

1 can (1 pound) red kidney beans
1 can (about 1 pound) stewed tomatoes
½ teaspoon salt
¼ teaspoon pepper
1 cup sliced pitted ripe olives

1 Sauté onion with chili powder in olive oil or vegetable oil just until onion is soft in a large frying pan; stir in remaining ingredients except olives; cover.
2 Simmer, stirring several times, 30 minutes to blend flavors; stir in olives.

Salty-Nut Topping
Makes about 1½ cups

¼ pound (1 stick) butter or margarine
1 can (8 ounces) walnuts, chopped
1 teaspoon seasoned salt

1 Melt butter or margarine in a small saucepan; stir in walnuts and seasoned salt.
2 Sauté, stirring often, 5 minutes, or until walnuts are buttery-hot.

Rarebit Topping
Makes about 3 cups

2 tablespoons butter or margarine
2 tablespoons flour
1 teaspoon salt
¼ teaspoon dry mustard
1 tablespoon Worcestershire sauce
2 cups milk
1 pound process American cheese, cut into pieces

1 Melt butter or margarine in a saucepan; blend in flour, salt, mustard, and Worcestershire sauce; cook just until bubbly. Stir in milk; continue cooking, stirring constantly, until sauce thickens and boils 1 minute.
2 Stir in cheese; cook, stirring constantly, just until cheese melts.

Spaghetti Topping
Makes about 7 cups

2 envelopes spaghetti-sauce mix
1 can (6 ounces) tomato paste
1 can (8 ounces) tomato sauce
4 tablespoons vegetable oil
3 cups water
1 package (8 ounces) thin spaghetti
½ cup grated Parmesan cheese

1 Blend spaghetti-sauce mix with tomato paste and tomato sauce in a large saucepan; stir in vegetable oil and water.
2 Heat to boiling; simmer, stirring once or twice, 25 to 30 minutes to blend flavors.
3 While sauce simmers, cook spaghetti, following label directions; drain. Spoon sauce over; sprinkle with cheese. Toss to mix well.

Skillet Enchiladas
Makes 8 servings

Sauce

3 medium-size onions, chopped (1½ cups)
1 tablespoon chili powder
2 tablespoons olive oil or vegetable oil
2 cans (about 1 pound each) tomatoes
2 cans (8 ounces each) tomato sauce
2 teaspoons sugar
1 teaspoon leaf oregano, crumbled
¼ teaspoon liquid red pepper seasoning
1 clove garlic

Tortillas and Filling

1 pound ground beef
1 teaspoon chili powder
1 clove garlic, minced
1 can (about 4 ounces) chopped ripe olives, drained
1 cup chopped green onions
¼ cup vegetable oil
8 tortillas (from an 11-ounce can)
1½ cups grated Cheddar cheese (6 ounces)

Topping

Sliced stuffed green olives
Sweet-onion rings

1 Make sauce: Sauté onions and chili powder in olive oil or vegetable oil until onions are soft in a large frying pan; stir in remaining sauce ingredients, sticking garlic onto a wooden pick so it will be easy to remove.
2 Simmer, adding a little water from time to time if mixture seems dry, 45 minutes to blend flavors; remove garlic.
3 Prepare tortillas: Mix ground beef lightly with chili powder and garlic; shape into a large patty in a medium-size frying pan. Brown 5 minutes on each side, then break up into chunks; remove from heat. Stir in ripe olives and green onions.
4 Heat vegetable oil in a small frying pan; dip

each tortilla into the hot oil just until softened. Remove and drain on paper toweling.

5 Spread each with a scant ⅓ cup meat mixture, then sprinkle with 1 tablespoon of the grated cheese. Roll up; place, spoke fashion and seam side down, in sauce in pan.

6 Spoon some of the sauce over rolls; sprinkle with remaining cheese.

7 Arrange topping: Place sliced green olives and onion rings on top of enchiladas; heat slowly just until enchiladas are hot and cheese melts slightly.

Hero's Hero

Bake at 425° for 25 minutes. Makes 6 servings

1 loaf Italian bread
1 pound meat-loaf mixture (ground beef, pork, and veal)
1 small onion, grated
1 teaspoon seasoned salt
¼ teaspoon leaf basil, crumbled
Dash of pepper
2 tablespoons butter or margarine
2 medium-size tomatoes, sliced ¼ inch thick
¼ teaspoon salt
¼ teaspoon leaf oregano, crumbled
1 cup shredded mozarella cheese
2 tablespoons grated Parmesan cheese

1 Slice bread lengthwise into 3 even layers. Place bottom and middle layers, cut sides up, on separate sheets of foil; tuck foil up around bread to cover crusts.

2 Combine meat-loaf mixture, onion, seasoned salt, basil, and pepper in a medium-size bowl; mix lightly until well-blended. Spread over bottom layer of bread to cover completely. Place on a large cooky sheet.

3 Spread middle and top layers of bread with butter or margarine; set top aside. Arrange tomato slices in a single layer over middle bread layer; sprinkle with salt, oregano, and mozzarella and Parmesan cheeses.

4 Bake meat layer in hot oven (425°) 10 minutes; place tomato layer on cooky sheet. Continue baking 12 minutes. Place top layer on cooky sheet; bake all 3 minutes longer, or until cheese melts.

5 Place meat layer on a cutting board; cover with tomato layer, then top of loaf, cut side down. Cut crosswise into thick slices with a sharp knife.

Pennsylvania Barbecue

These saucy burgers are so popular they boast many countrywide variations

Makes 6 servings

½ pound sausage meat
1½ pounds ground beef
1 large onion, chopped (1 cup)
1 cup diced celery
1 bottle (12 ounces) chili sauce
1 can (8 ounces) tomato sauce
1½ cups water
2 tablespoons prepared mustard
1 teaspoon celery salt
1 teaspoon salt
¼ teaspoon pepper
6 toasted, split hamburger rolls

1 Sauté sausage 3 to 5 minutes in large kettle or Dutch oven; remove and set aside. Drain all but 1 tablespoon fat from kettle.

2 Press ground beef into a large patty in same kettle; brown 5 minutes. Cut into quarters; turn; brown other side 5 minutes, then break up into chunks; push to one side. Add onion and celery; sauté just until soft.

3 Return sausage to kettle; stir in remaining ingredients, except rolls. Simmer, uncovered, stirring often, 45 minutes, or until thick.

4 Butter rolls, if you like; spoon hot meat mixture over.

●

Dinner Beef Patties

Makes 4 servings

1 large Bermuda onion
2 tablespoons butter or margarine
¼ cup water
3 tablespoons brown sugar
Paprika
2 pounds ground beef
2 teaspoons salt
CHILI GLAZE *(recipe follows)*

1 Peel onion and cut crosswise into 4 thick slices. Sauté in butter or margarine until lightly browned on bottom; turn carefully; add water and brown sugar; cover. Simmer 10 minutes, or just until tender; sprinkle with paprika. Keep hot while fixing and cooking meat.

2 Mix ground beef lightly with salt; shape into 4 large and 4 medium-size patties about 1 inch thick.

3 Pan-fry over medium heat 8 minutes; turn;

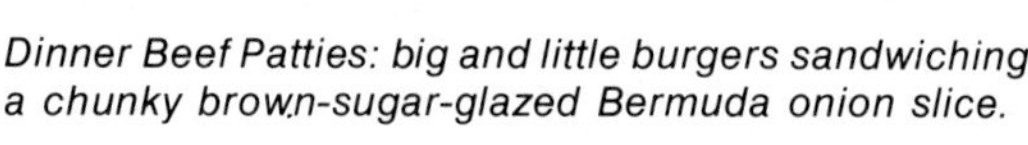

Dinner Beef Patties: big and little burgers sandwiching a chunky brown-sugar-glazed Bermuda onion slice.

cook 5 minutes longer. Spoon CHILI GLAZE over; continue cooking, basting with glaze in pan, 3 minutes longer for medium, or until meat is done as you like it.

4 Put one each large and medium-size patty together with a Bermuda-onion slice between on a serving plate. Top with any remaining sauce from pan.

CHILI GLAZE—Combine ½ cup chili sauce with ½ cup water, 1 tablespoon corn syrup, and 1 tablespoon Worcestershire sauce in a 2-cup measure. Makes about 1 cup.

Torpedoes

Makes 6 servings

2 pounds ground beef
1 can (about 10 ounces) pizza sauce
1 teaspoon salt
¼ teaspoon pepper
¼ teaspoon leaf oregano, crumbled
1 package (6 ounces) sliced provolone cheese, cut in strips
1 tablespoon vegetable oil
6 split frankfurter rolls, toasted

1 Combine ground beef, ⅓ cup of the pizza sauce, salt, pepper, and oregano in a medium-size bowl; mix lightly until well-blended. Divide into 6 even mounds.

2 Pat each mound into a 6-inch round on wax paper or foil; top one half of each with cheese strips, dividing evenly. Fold other half of round over cheese to cover completely, then shape into an oval about 6 inches long to fit frankfurter rolls.

3 Brown in vegetable oil in a large frying pan; spoon all fat from pan. Pour remaining pizza sauce over meat; cover. Simmer 20 minutes.

4 Place a meat roll in each frankfurter roll. Skim any fat from remaining sauce in pan. Serve separately to spoon over sandwiches.

Slumgullion-on-a-Bun

Makes 8 servings

2 pounds ground beef
1 large onion, chopped (1 cup)
1 clove garlic, minced
1 envelope spaghetti-sauce mix
1 can (1 pint, 2 ounces) tomato juice
1 cup chopped celery
1 can (12 or 16 ounces) whole-kernel corn
½ cup chopped dill pickle
8 split hamburger buns

1 Shape ground beef into a large patty in a kettle or Dutch oven. Brown 5 minutes on each side, then break up into chunks; push to one side.

2 Add onion and garlic; sauté just until soft. Stir in spaghetti-sauce mix, tomato juice, celery, and corn and liquid; cover.

3 Simmer 30 minutes, or until thick; stir in chopped pickle.

4 Spoon over hamburger buns. Top with chopped sweet onions or grated cheese, if you wish.

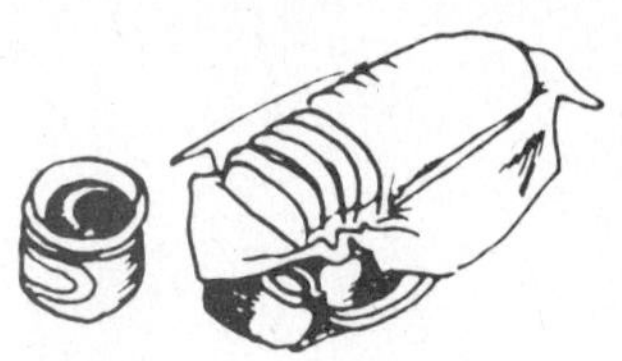

Greek Lamb Patties

Makes 4 to 6 servings

1 medium-size onion, chopped (½ cup)
2 tablespoons vegetable oil
2 pounds ground lamb
1 teaspoon salt
Dash of pepper
2 teaspoons dried mint flakes
½ cup fine dry bread crumbs
1 cup tomato juice
1 can (13 ounces) chicken broth
Water
1 tablespoon cornstarch
2 eggs
3 tablespoons lemon juice

1 Sauté onion in 1 tablespoon of the vegetable oil until soft in a large frying pan.

2 Combine lamb with salt, pepper, mint, bread crumbs, tomato juice, and onion mixture in a large bowl; mix lightly until well-blended. Shape into 8 patties about ¾ inch thick.

3 Brown patties slowly in remaining 1 tablespoon vegetable oil in same frying pan, turning once, 20 minutes.

4 While lamb cooks, pour chicken broth into a 2-cup measure; add water to make 2 cups. Blend a small amount into cornstarch until smooth in a medium-size saucepan, then stir in remainder. Cook, stirring constantly, until mixture thickens and boils 3 minutes.

5 Beat eggs until light in a small bowl; blend in about half of the hot chicken sauce, then stir back into remaining sauce in pan. Cook, stirring constantly, 1 minute longer; remove from heat. Stir in lemon juice. Serve separately to spoon over lamb patties.

Lamb In Dill Gravy
Makes 6 servings

2 *pounds ground lamb*
2 *teaspoons salt*
¼ *teaspoon liquid red pepper seasoning*
6 *medium-size zucchini, trimmed and cut in 1-inch cubes*
4 *tablespoons (½ stick) butter or margarine*
¼ *cup sifted all-purpose flour*
1½ *teaspoons dillweed*
1 *teaspoon salt*
3 *cups milk*

1 Break up lamb and combine with salt and red pepper seasoning in a large bowl; mix lightly until well-blended. Shape into 6 patties about ½ inch thick.
2 Pan-fry slowly, turning once, in a large frying pan 12 minutes for medium. Place on a deep serving platter; keep warm.
3 While lamb cooks, cook zucchini in boiling salted water in a large saucepan 10 minutes, or just until tender; drain well. Arrange around lamb on platter.
4 Pour all drippings from frying pan, then melt butter or margarine in same pan. Blend in flour; cook, stirring constantly, until bubbly. Stir in dillweed, salt, and milk; continue cooking and stirring until sauce thickens and boils 1 minute. Drizzle part over lamb and zucchini; serve remainder separately.

Veal Patties Cordon Bleu
Makes 6 servings

2 *pounds ground veal*
1 *packet (2 to an envelope) green-onion dip mix*
2 *long slices Swiss cheese, cut in thirds*
3 *slices boiled ham (from a 6-ounce package), halved*
2 *eggs*
1 *cup fine dry bread crumbs*
1 *tablespoon butter or margarine*
1 *tablespoon vegetable oil*

1 Combine veal and dip mix in a large bowl; mix lightly until well-blended. Divide into 12 even mounds. Pat out each to a rectangle, 4x3, on wax paper or foil.
2 Top each of 6 meat rectangles with a piece of cheese, then a piece of ham, folding, if needed, to fit. Cover each with a remaining meat rectangle; press the edges together to seal.
3 Beat eggs slightly in a pie plate; sprinkle bread crumbs on wax paper. Dip each patty into beaten egg, then into bread crumbs to coat well.
4 Sauté slowly in butter or margarine and vegetable oil, turning once, in a large frying pan, 8 minutes on each side, or until crispy-brown and cooked through.

Mock Drumsticks
Bake at 400° for 40 minutes. Makes 8 servings

2 *pounds ground veal*
1 *egg*
½ *cup milk*
1½ *cups cracker meal*
2 *teaspoons salt*
½ *teaspoon pepper*
½ *teaspoon leaf sage, crumbled*
¾ *cup (1½ sticks) butter or margarine*

1 Combine ground veal, egg, milk, ½ cup of the cracker meal, salt, pepper, and sage in a large bowl; mix lightly.
2 Divide into 16 equal mounds; form each into a drumstick shape around a wooden skewer.
3 Melt butter or margarine in a small frying pan; sprinkle remaining 1 cup cracker meal on wax paper. Dip each drumstick into melted butter, then roll in cracker meal. Place in a single layer in a well-greased jelly-roll pan. Drizzle remaining melted butter or margarine over tops.
4 Bake in hot oven (400°), turning once, 40 minutes, or until golden.

Sweet-Sour Ham-Burgers
Bake at 400° for 30 minutes. Makes 4 servings

1 *can (12 ounces) pork luncheon meat*
¼ *pound process American cheese*
½ *cup quick-cooking rolled oats*
1 *egg, slightly beaten*
1 *tablespoon butter or margarine*
1 *tablespoon brown sugar*
1 *tablespoon cornstarch*
1 *cup water*
1 *can (14 ounces) pineapple chunks*
1 *tablespoon vinegar*
¼ *teaspoon ginger*

1 Put pork luncheon meat and cheese through food chopper, using coarse knife.
2 Combine ground meat-cheese mixture, rolled oats, and egg in medium size bowl; blend with 2-tine fork.

3 Form mixture into 8 large balls; place in shallow baking pan.
4 Bake in hot oven (400°) 20 minutes, or until brown and crusty.
5 While meat balls brown, heat butter or margarine in medium-size saucepan; blend in brown sugar and cornstarch; gradually stir in water, pineapple and syrup, vinegar, and ginger.
6 Cook, stirring constantly, until sauce thickens and boils 1 minute.
7 Remove meat balls from oven; drain fat from pan.
8 Spoon sauce over and around meat balls; return to oven; bake 10 minutes longer to blend flavors.

MEAT BALLS

Party Meat Balls

Deviled ham adds extra spice to these saucy little beef-and-veal balls
Makes 12 servings

1½ pounds ground beef
1 pound ground veal
1 can (4½ ounces) deviled ham
1 small can evaporated milk (⅔ cup)
2 eggs
1 tablespoon grated onion
1 cup soft whole-wheat bread crumbs (2 slices)
½ teaspoon salt
½ teaspoon ground allspice
¼ teaspoon pepper
¼ cup vegetable shortening
¼ cup water
Creamy Dill Sauce (recipe follows)

1 Combine ground beef and veal, deviled ham, evaporated milk, eggs, onion, bread crumbs, and seasonings in large bowl; mix lightly with a fork. Shape into about 72 small balls.
2 Brown, a few at a time, in vegetable shortening in large frying pan. Drain any fat from pan; return meat balls. Add water; cover. Simmer 20 minutes, or until heated through. (If made ahead, chill after browning, then reheat with water in frying pan just before serving.)
3 Spoon into a chafing dish or keep-hot server. Pour *Creamy Dill Sauce* over. Garnish with a sprig of fresh dill, if you like.

Crowd Coming? Do Party Meat Balls, serve on a buffet.

Creamy Dill Sauce

Make the base ahead, if you wish, ready to stir in sour cream and seasonings and heat just before serving
Makes about 2 cups

2 tablespoons butter or margarine
2 tablespoons flour
½ teaspoon salt
1 cup water
1 cup dairy sour cream
1 tablespoon catsup
1 tablespoon dillweed

1 Melt butter or margarine in small saucepan; blend in flour and salt; cook, stirring all the time, just until mixture bubbles. Stir in water slowly; continue cooking and stirring until sauce thickens and boils 1 minute.
2 Stir in sour cream, catsup, and dillweed; heat just to boiling.

Tureen Beef Balls

Makes 6 servings

1 pound ground beef
¾ cup fine dry bread crumbs
1 egg
3 teaspoons salt
¼ teaspoon pepper
¼ teaspoon leaf basil, crumbled
1 cup chopped celery
1 medium-size onion, chopped (½ cup)
4 tablespoons (½ stick) butter or margarine
3 cans (10½ ounces each) condensed beef broth
4 cups water
1 can (1 pound) tomatoes
2 cups diced pared parsnips
1 package (10 ounces) frozen succotash
3 tablespoons chopped parsley

1 Combine ground beef, bread crumbs, egg, 1 teaspoon of the salt, pepper, and basil in a medium-size bowl; mix lightly until well-blended. Shape into 24 balls.
2 Sauté celery and onion in butter or margarine until soft in a kettle; stir in beef broth, water, tomatoes and juice, and remaining 2 teaspoons salt. Heat to boiling; add meat balls. Simmer, stirring several times, 15 minutes. Stir in parsnips and succotash.
3 Simmer 15 minutes longer, or until all vegetables are tender. Stir in chopped parsley.
4 Ladle into heated soup bowls. Serve with toasted hard rolls or French bread, if you wish.

Platter Stew

Meat balls, two vegetables, and gravy go into this colorful main dish that cooks in one pan
Makes 4 servings

- *1 pound ground beef*
- *1 can (10½ ounces) condensed beef broth*
- *¼ cup fine dry crumbs*
- *1 small onion, grated*
- *1 teaspoon salt*
- *⅛ teaspoon pepper*
- *2 tablespoons butter or margarine*
- *3 medium-size yellow squashes, trimmed and sliced 1 inch thick*
- *8 small carrots, pared*
- *½ cup evaporated milk*
- *1 tablespoon instant-type flour*

1 Combine ground beef, ¼ cup of the beef broth, bread crumbs, onion, salt, and pepper in a medium-size bowl; mix lightly with a fork. Shape into 20 small balls.
2 Brown in butter or margarine in a Dutch oven or a large frying pan; pour remaining broth over. Place squashes and carrots around meat balls; cover. Simmer 25 minutes, or until vegetables are tender.
3 Remove meat balls with a slotted spoon and place in center of a deep serving platter; place vegetables around edge.
4 Blend evaporated milk and flour in a cup; stir into hot liquid in pan. Cook, stirring constantly, until gravy thickens and boils 1 minute. Spoon over meat and vegetables.

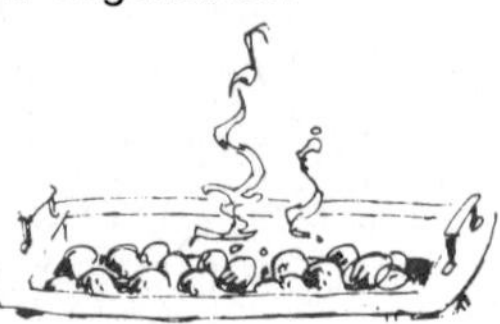

Hawaiian Burger Balls

Makes 8 servings

- *2 pounds ground beef*
- *1 egg*
- *½ cup chopped walnuts*
- *2 teaspoons salt*
- *¼ teaspoon pepper*
- *¼ teaspoon ground ginger*
- *¼ cup vegetable oil*
- *2 large onions, peeled and sliced*
- *1 can (about 1 pound, 14 ounces) sliced pineapple*
- *3 tablespoons soy sauce*
- *2 tablespoons molasses*
- *4 tablespoons cornstarch*
- *¼ cup water*
- *1 large green pepper, quartered, seeded, and cut in bite-size pieces*
- *¼ cup cider vinegar*

1 Combine ground beef, egg, walnuts, salt, pepper, and ginger in a large bowl; mix lightly until well-blended. Shape into 16 balls.
2 Brown in vegetable oil in a large frying pan; remove with a slotted spoon and set aside.
3 Stir onions into drippings in frying pan; sauté just until soft.
4 Drain syrup from pineapple into a 2-cup measure; add water to make 2 cups. Halve 3 of the pineapple slices and set aside for garnish; dice remaining.
5 Stir syrup mixture into frying pan with soy sauce and molasses; heat to boiling. Place meat balls in sauce; cover. Simmer 15 minutes.
6 Smooth cornstarch to a paste with water in a cup; stir into meat-ball mixture. Cook, stirring constantly, until sauce thickens and boils 3 minutes.
7 Stir in green pepper, diced pineapple, and vinegar. Heat slowly just until bubbly. Spoon into a heated serving dish; stand halved pineapple slices around edge. Serve with fluffy hot rice, if you wish.

Baked Saucy Meat Balls

Bake at 375° for 1 hour. Makes 8 servings

- *1½ pounds ground beef*
- *½ pound sausage meat*
- *1 jar (8 ounces) junior applesauce*
- *1 cup soft bread crumbs (2 slices)*
- *8 prunes, pitted and chopped*
- *1 teaspoon salt*
- *¼ teaspoon pepper*
- *1 can (10¾ ounces) condensed tomato soup*
- *¼ cup water*

1 Combine ground beef, sausage meat, applesauce, bread crumbs, prunes, salt, and pepper in a large bowl. Mix lightly with a fork just until blended. Shape into 24 balls. Place in an 8-cup baking dish.
2 Blend tomato soup and water in a small bowl; pour over meat balls; cover.
3 Bake in moderate oven (375°) 1 hour, or until bubbly in center.

Swedish Meatballs

Shape the meat with a gentle touch so it will stay fluffy-tender during cooking
Bake at 325° for 30 minutes. Makes 6 servings

- *3 slices white bread, crumbled*
- *1 tablespoon instant minced onion*
- *1½ teaspoons salt*

For an impressive but economical entrée, try serving Beef Rolls Cordon Bleu.

- *¼ teaspoon pepper*
- *¼ teaspoon ground nutmeg*
- *¾ cup milk*
- *2 pounds meat-loaf mixture (ground beef, pork and veal)*
- *4 tablespoons (½ stick) butter or margarine*
- *2 tablespoons flour*
- *1 can (10½ ounces) condensed beef broth*
- *1 cup light cream or table cream*

1 Combine bread, onion, salt, pepper, nutmeg, and milk in a large bowl; let stand 10 minutes.
2 Stir in meat-loaf mixture until well-blended; form into 1½-inch balls. Brown in butter or margarine in a large frying pan. Remove with a slotted spoon and place in a 10-cup baking dish.
3 Blend flour into drippings in pan; cook, stirring constantly, until bubbly. Stir in beef broth and cream; continue cooking and stirring until sauce thickens and boils 1 minute; pour over meat balls.
4 Bake in slow oven (325°) 30 minutes.

Tivoli Meat Balls

Makes 4 servings

- *¾ pound ground beef*
- *¼ pound ground fresh pork*
- *1 cup soft bread crumbs (2 slices, no crusts)*
- *1 onion, grated*
- *1 egg*
- *½ cup milk*
- *1 teaspoon salt*
- *¼ teaspoon ground nutmeg*
- *⅛ teaspoon pepper*
- *2 cups water*
- *½ cup junior-pack chopped prunes (from an 8-ounce jar)*

1 Mix meats, bread crumbs, onion, egg, milk, and seasonings in medium-size bowl; form lightly with fingers into marble-size balls (you'll get between 40 and 50).
2 Heat water and prunes to boiling in frying pan; add meat balls; cover; simmer 20 minutes, turning once.
3 Serve over seasoned hot rice or mashed potatoes.

Beef Rolls Cordon Bleu

Cosmopolitan choice has Swiss cheese and Canadian bacon layered inside
Makes 8 servings

- *3 pounds ground beef*
- *1 teaspoon salt*

- 1 teaspoon dried vegetable flakes
- 1 package (8 ounces) sliced Swiss cheese, halved crosswise
- 1 package (6 ounces) sliced Canadian bacon
- 2 eggs
- ¼ cup water
- 1 cup seasoned bread crumbs (from a 10-ounce package)
- ⅓ cup butter or margarine
- 1 can (10½ ounces) condensed golden mushroom soup
- 1 cup milk
- 1 medium-size tomato, cut in 8 wedges

1 Mix ground beef lightly with salt and vegetable flakes in a large bowl; shape into 8 patties about ¼-inch thick. Top each with a slice of cheese and Canadian bacon; roll up, jelly-roll fashion.
2 Beat eggs with water in a pie plate; place bread crumbs in a second pie plate. Dip meat rolls into egg mixture, then into bread crumbs to coat well.
3 Sauté, turning often, in butter or margarine in a large frying pan 25 minutes, or until beef is done as you like it. Remove to a heated serving platter; keep warm while making gravy.
4 Pour all drippings from frying pan, then stir soup and milk into pan. Heat slowly, stirring constantly and scraping brown bits from bottom of pan, until bubbly hot. Taste and season with salt and pepper, if needed.
5 Garnish meat rolls with tomato wedges; serve with gravy, and parslied potatoes and buttered green beans, if you wish.

Highland Dinner

Meat and vegetables cook lazily, so it's a good choice for a stay-at-home day.
Bake at 300° for 2 hours and 20 minutes, then at 425° for 20 minutes. Makes 8 servings

- ½ pound link sausages
- 2 pounds ground beef or lamb
- 6 tablespoons all-purpose flour

Ground meat and sausages team in Highland dinner.

2 teaspoons salt
¼ teaspoon pepper
1 medium-size onion, chopped
1 envelope instant beef broth
OR: 1 beef-flavor bouillon cube
¼ cup bottled chili sauce
¼ teaspoon leaf marjoram, crumbled
¼ teaspoon leaf rosemary, crumbled
3 cups water
8 medium-size carrots, pared, halved lengthwise, and cut in 1-inch lengths
4 medium-size potatoes, pared and cut up
1 package (9 ounces) frozen cut green beans
1½ cups biscuit mix
½ cup grated Cheddar cheese
½ cup milk

1 Slice sausages ½ inch thick; brown slowly in a large frying pan; remove with a slotted spoon and set aside in a bowl.
2 Shape ground beef or lamb into 1-inch balls, then roll in a mixture of flour, salt, and pepper to coat well. Brown in drippings in same pan; remove and add to sausage.
3 Stir onion into pan and sauté until soft; stir in browned meat, beef broth or bouillon cube, chili sauce, marjoram, rosemary, and water; heat, stirring constantly, to boiling. Spoon into a 12-cup baking dish. Stir in carrots, potatoes, and beans, breaking up beans with a fork; cover.
4 Bake in slow oven (300°) 2 hours and 20 minutes; remove from oven; raise temperature to hot (425°). Skim any fat from meat mixture.
5 Combine biscuit mix and cheese in a medium-size bowl; add milk all at once; stir lightly just until evenly moist. Turn out onto a lightly floured pastry cloth or board; knead ½ minute. Roll out to a rectangle, 10x6; cut crosswise into 8 strips about ¾ inch wide with a pastry wheel or knife. Weave strips over meat mixture to make a crisscross top.
6 Bake in hot oven (425°) 20 minutes, or until golden-brown.

Belgian Beef Balls
Makes 6 servings

1½ pounds ground beef
½ cup soft bread crumbs (1 slice)
2 cans (10½ ounces each) condensed beef broth
½ cup sifted all-purpose flour
2 tablespoons vegetable oil
1 large onion, peeled and sliced
1 can (12 ounces) beer
½ teaspoon leaf thyme, crumbled
½ teaspoon garlic salt
¼ teaspoon pepper
¼ cup water
1 tablespoon chopped parsley

1 Mix ground beef with bread crumbs and ½ cup of the beef broth in a large bowl; shape into 12 large balls.
2 Measure 6 tablespoons of the flour onto wax paper; roll meat balls in flour to coat; lightly tap off any excess.
3 Sauté meat balls in vegetable oil until richly browned in a large frying pan; remove from pan; keep warm. Pour off all drippings, then measure 2 tablespoonfuls and return to pan.
4 Stir in onion; sauté until soft. Stir in remaining beef broth, beer, thyme, garlic salt, and pepper; heat to boiling; simmer 5 minutes.
5 Blend remaining 2 tablespoons flour and water to a paste in a cup; stir into liquid in frying pan. Cook, stirring constantly, until gravy thickens and boils 1 minute.
6 Place meat balls in gravy; cover. Simmer 10 minutes.
7 Spoon meat balls and gravy onto a heated deep serving platter; sprinkle with parsley. Serve with cooked noodles or boiled potatoes, if you wish.

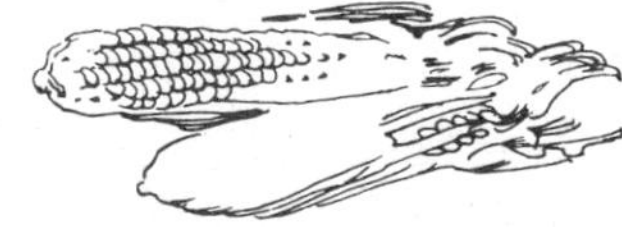

Beef Burgundy
Makes 6 servings

1½ pounds ground beef
1 egg
½ cup soft bread crumbs (1 slice)
¼ cup milk
1½ teaspoons salt
½ teaspoon garlic salt
3 tablespoons butter or margarine
1 pound small white onions, peeled
1 pound small mushrooms, trimmed
1 teaspoon sugar
⅓ cup sifted all-purpose flour
1 can (10½ ounces) condensed beef broth
1 cup dry red wine
1 medium-size carrot, pared and sliced
1 bay leaf

1 Combine ground beef, egg, bread crumbs, milk, 1 teaspoon of the salt, and garlic salt in a large bowl; mix lightly until well-blended. Shape into 12 balls.
2 Melt butter or margarine in a kettle or Dutch oven; add onions and mushrooms; sprinkle with sugar. Brown quickly; remove with a slotted spoon to a shallow pan.
3 Add meat balls to drippings in kettle; brown. Combine with vegetables.

4 Blend flour and remaining ½ teaspoon salt into drippings in kettle; stir in beef broth until smooth, then wine and carrot. Heat, stirring constantly, to boiling. Stir in bay leaf, onions, mushrooms, and meat balls; cover. Simmer 35 minutes; remove bay leaf.
5 Spoon mixture into a heated serving dish. Sprinkle with chopped parsley, if you wish.

Cooksaver tip:

Flouring meat balls? Speed up the job by sprinkling the flour from a shaker, or toss the meat balls, a few at a time, in flour in a paper bag to coat well. Place salt, pepper, spices, or herb seasonings in the bag, too—another time-saver step.

Königsberg Meat Balls

(Königsberger Klops)
Makes 8 servings

4 slices bread
½ cup milk
2 pounds meat-loaf mixture (ground beef, pork and veal)
1 can (2 ounces) anchovy fillets, drained and chopped
3 eggs
1 small onion, grated
2 tablespoons grated lemon rind
1 teaspoon salt
¼ teaspoon pepper
2 envelopes instant beef broth or 1 teaspoon granulated beef bouillon
4 cups water
¼ cup (½ stick) butter or margarine
¼ cup sifted all-purpose flour
1 teaspoon sugar
½ cup dry white wine
2 tablespoons well-drained capers
1 tablespoon lemon juice

1 Place bread slices in single layer in a shallow dish; pour milk over; let stand until absorbed (about 10 minutes); break apart with fork into small pieces.
2 Combine meat-loaf mixture, half the anchovies, eggs, onion, lemon rind, salt, pepper, and bread in a large bowl, mixing lightly. Shape into 32 balls.
3 Combine beef broth and water in a large skillet; heat to boiling; add meat balls, lowering into boiling broth with a slotted spoon. Simmer, uncovered, 15 minutes, or until no longer pink in center (break one open to test). Remove with slotted spoon to a deep platter. Reserve cooking liquid.
4 Make sauce: Melt butter or margarine in a medium-size saucepan; stir in flour and sugar; cook until bubbly, stirring constantly. Gradually add wine and 2 cups of the cooking liquid, continuing to stir until mixture is thickened and bubbles 1 minute. Stir in capers, lemon juice, and remaining half of anchovies, stirring until anchovies are blended into sauce. Spoon over meat balls. Serve with sauerkraut and mashed or boiled potatoes, if you wish.

Meat Balls Caribe

Makes 6 servings

1½ pounds ground beef
1 teaspoon grated lime rind
6 slices bacon, diced
1 large onion, chopped (1 cup)
1 can (10½ ounces) condensed beef broth
1 cup water
1½ teaspoons salt
⅛ teaspoon cayenne
1 bay leaf
6 medium-size potatoes, peeled and quartered
2 tablespoons flour
2 large green peppers, halved, seeded, and chopped
2 large ripe tomatoes, peeled and quartered
¼ cup ripe olives, sliced

1 Mix ground beef lightly with lime rind. Shape with tablespoon into 35 small balls.
2 Sauté bacon until crisp in a large skillet; remove.
3 Brown meat balls, half at a time, in bacon drippings; remove with a slotted spoon; reserve.
4 Drain all but 2 tablespoons of the drippings from skillet, then sauté onions just until soft.
5 Stir beef broth, water, salt, cayenne, and bay leaf into drippings in skillet. return meat balls; cover. Simmer 10 minutes.
6 Add potatoes; simmer 20 minutes, or until almost done.

7 Remove meat balls and potatoes with a slotted spoon. Remove and discard bay leaf. Stir about ½ cup of the cooking liquid into flour until smooth in a small cup, then stir back into remaining liquid in skillet. Cook, stirring constantly, until gravy thickens and bubbles 1 minute.
8 Return meat balls and potatoes to skillet. Add green pepper, tomatoes, and olives; cover; reduce heat. Simmer 10 minutes longer. Top with crisp bacon.

Beef Balls Stroganoff
Wheat germ takes the place of bread crumbs, adds flavor and protein
Makes 8 servings

2 pounds ground beef
1 cup regular wheat germ
2 eggs
1 cup dairy sour cream
½ cup finely chopped onion
1½ teaspoons salt
4 tablespoons bottled steak sauce
1 can (8 ounces) stewed tomatoes

1 Combine ground beef, wheat germ, eggs, ½ cup of the sour cream, onion, salt, and 1 tablespoon steak sauce in a large bowl; mix until well-blended. Shape into 1-inch balls.
2 Brown in a large frying pan; remove.
3 Stir remaining 3 tablespoons steak sauce and tomatoes into drippings in pan; return meatballs; cover. Simmer 15 minutes. Remove with a slotted spoon to a large deep serving platter; keep warm.
4 Stir about ¼ cup of the hot sauce into remaining ½ cup sour cream in a small bowl; stir back into sauce in pan. Heat *very slowly* just until hot; spoon over meatballs. Garnish with watercress.

Rancho Beef Dinner
One pound ground beef and a little bacon for seasoning make this satisfying casserole
Bake at 350° for 40 minutes. Makes 6 servings

1 cup yellow cornmeal
6 slices bacon
1 pound ground beef
1½ teaspoons salt
⅛ teaspoon pepper
¼ cup chopped parsley
1 large onion, chopped (1 cup)
½ cup chopped celery
½ clove garlic, crushed
1 can (about 1 pound) tomatoes
1 package (6 ounces) cubed Cheddar cheese

1 Prepare cornmeal, following label directions for cornmeal mush; pour into a greased baking dish, 13x9x2; chill.
2 Sauté bacon until crisp in a medium-size frying pan; drain on paper toweling. Crumble and set aside for Step 6. Pour off drippings, then measure 2 tablespoonfuls and return to pan.
3 Mix ground beef, 1 teaspoon of the salt, pepper, and parsley in a medium-size bowl. (Remaining ½ teaspoon salt is for sauce in next step.) Shape meat into 24 small balls; brown in drippings in pan, then remove; set aside for Step 6.
4 Sauté onion, celery, and garlic just until soft in same pan; stir in tomatoes, cheese, and remaining ½ teaspoon salt. Remove from heat.
5 Remove chilled cornmeal mush from pan by turning upside down on a cutting board; cut into about 1½-inch cubes.
6 Set aside about 10 for top, then place half of the remaining in the bottom of a greased 10-cup baking dish. Top with half each of the meat balls and sauce and crumbled bacon. Repeat to make another layer of each, mounding meat balls in center; arrange saved cornmeal cubes around edge.
7 Bake in moderate oven (350°) 40 minutes, or until bubbly hot.

Cabbage Roll-Ups
Bake at 375° for 45 minutes. Makes 4 servings

8 large cabbage leaves (from a medium-size head)
1 pound ground beef
¼ cup quick-cooking rolled oats
1 small onion, chopped (¼ cup)
1 tablespoon chopped parsley
1 egg
1 can (10½ ounces) condensed beef broth
1 teaspoon salt
⅛ teaspoon pepper
1 tablespoon butter or margarine

1 Trim base of cabbage and carefully break off

8 whole leaves. (Save remaining cabbage to cook for a vegetable or make into salad for another meal.)

2 Place leaves in a large saucepan; pour in water to a depth of 1 inch; cover. Heat to boiling; remove from heat. Let stand 5 minutes, or until leaves wilt; drain well.

3 Mix ground beef lightly with rolled oats, onion, parsley, egg, ⅔ cup of the beef broth, salt, and pepper until well-blended.

4 Lay cabbage leaves flat on counter top; spoon meat mixture onto middle of each, dividing evenly. Fold edges of each leaf over filling and roll up; fasten with wooden picks. Arrange rolls in a single layer in a greased shallow 6-cup baking dish.

5 Pour remaining broth over cabbage rolls; dot with butter or margarine; cover.

6 Bake in moderate oven (375°) 45 minutes, or until cabbage is tender. Lift onto a heated serving platter with a slotted spoon; remove picks. Serve sauce separately to spoon over rolls, if you wish. Or arrange cabbage rolls on top of a platter of hot cooked noodles; spoon sauce over. Garnish with a kebab of pitted ripe olives and a sweet yellow wax pepper.

Speedy Party Lasagna

Bake at 425° for 25 minutes. Makes 12 servings

2 packages (1 pound, 8 ounces each) lasagna dinner
2 packages (10 ounces each) frozen chopped spinach
1 pound ground beef
2 cups (1-pound carton) cream-style cottage cheese
1 egg
2 teaspoons Italian seasoning
½ teaspoon salt

1 Cook noodles from packages of lasagna dinner, following label directions; drain.

2 Cook spinach, following label directions; drain.

3 Shape ground beef into a patty in a frying pan; brown 5 minutes on each side, then break up into chunks. Stir in sauce from lasagna dinner.

4 Mix cottage cheese with egg, Italian seasoning, and salt; stir in spinach.

5 Set aside 6 noodles. Layer half of remaining noodles, cheese mixture, meat sauce, and grated cheese (from packages) into a greased baking dish, 13x9x2. Repeat layers.

6 Roll up saved noodles, jelly-roll fashion; slice in half and press, cut sides down, into sauce.

7 Bake in hot oven (425°) 25 minutes, or until bubbly hot.

Veal Fricassee

Makes 6 servings

2 pounds ground veal
1½ cups soft bread crumbs (3 slices)
1 medium-size onion, chopped (½ cup)
1 egg
½ cup milk
2 tablespoons lemon juice
1 tablespoon chopped parsley
1 teaspoon garlic salt
¼ teaspoon ground thyme
Water
1 bay leaf
½ teaspoon celery seeds
1 can (1 pound) small whole onions
1 jar (1 pound) chunk-style carrots
2 tablespoons butter or margarine
2 tablespoons flour
1 cup light cream or table cream
1 egg yolk

1 Combine veal, bread crumbs, onion, egg, milk, 1 tablespoon of the lemon juice, parsley, garlic salt, and thyme in a large bowl; mix lightly until well-blended. Shape into 1-inch balls.

2 Heat 6 cups water to boiling in a large frying pan; season with bay leaf and celery seeds. Add veal balls, half at a time; simmer 8 minutes, or until cooked through. Remove with a slotted spoon to a deep serving platter; keep warm.

3 Strain cooking liquid into a bowl, then measure 1 cupful and set aside for sauce; discard remainder.

4 Heat onions and carrots in their liquids in separate small saucepans 10 minutes, or until hot; drain. Place in mounds around veal on platter.

5 Melt butter or margarine in same frying pan; stir in flour. Cook, stirring constantly, until bubbly. Stir in the saved 1 cup liquid and cream; continue cooking and stirring until sauce thickens and boils 1 minute.

6 Beat about 1 cup of the hot mixture into egg yolk in a small bowl, then slowly stir back into remaining mixture in pan. Cook, stirring constantly, 1 minute longer; remove from heat. Stir in remaining 1 tablespoon lemon juice; season with salt, if needed. Spoon over veal balls and vegetables.

Meat Balls Scandia

Bake at 450° for 20 minutes, then at 350° for 15 minutes. Makes 8 servings

1 pound ground veal
1 pound ground beef
1 large tart apple, pared, quartered, cored, and grated
1 small onion, grated
2 cups soft bread crumbs (4 slices)
3 eggs
¼ cup chopped parsley
2 teaspoons seasoned salt
1 teaspoon ground ginger
Dill Gravy (recipe follows)

1 Combine all ingredients (except *Dill Gravy*) in large bowl; mix lightly with a fork just until blended. Shape into 48 small balls; place in single layer in greased large shallow baking pan.
2 Bake in very hot oven (450°), turning balls once, 20 minutes, or until lightly browned. Remove with slotted spoon and mound in the middle of a shallow 8-cup baking dish.
3 Reduce oven heat to moderate (350°); slide dish into oven to keep hot while making *Dill Gravy.* Pour gravy around meat balls; cover.
4 Bake in moderate oven (350°) 15 minutes to blend flavors. Garnish with a few sprigs of parsley, if you wish.

DILL GRAVY—Pour 2⅓ cups hot water into baking pan; stir to mix with drippings and baked-on meat juices. Strain into a 4-cup measure. Melt 4 tablespoons (½ stick) butter or margarine in medium-size saucepan; blend in 6 tablespoons all-purpose flour and 1 teaspoon salt; cook, stirring all the time, just until mixture bubbles. Slowly stir in drippings mixture and 1 tall can evaporated milk; continue cooking

Proving the versatility of ground beef: Cabbage Roll-Ups, Rancho Beef Dinner and Speedy Party Lasagna.

and stirring until gravy thickens and boils 1 minute; stir in 2 teaspoons dillweed. Makes 4 cups.

Saucy Dill Meat Balls

Makes 10 to 12 servings

Meat Balls

1½ pounds ground beef
1 pound ground veal
1 can (4½ ounces) deviled ham
1 small can evaporated milk (⅔ cup)
2 eggs
1 cup soft whole-wheat bread crumbs (2 slices)
1 small onion, grated
½ teaspoon salt
¼ teaspoon ground cloves
¼ teaspoon pepper
¼ cup vegetable shortening
¼ cup water

Sauce

2 tablespoons butter or margarine
2 tablespoons all-purpose flour
½ teaspoon salt
1 cup water
1 cup (8-ounce carton) dairy sour cream
1 tablespoon catsup
1 tablespoon dill weed

1 Make meat balls: Mix ground beef and veal and deviled ham lightly with evaporated milk, eggs, bread crumbs, onion, and seasonings until well-blended; shape into 72 balls.
2 Brown, a few at a time, in shortening in a large frying pan; pour off all drippings. Return all meat balls to pan; add water; cover. Simmer 20 minutes, or until cooked through.
3 Make sauce: Melt butter or margarine in a small saucepan; blend in flour and salt; stir in water. Cook, stirring constantly, until sauce thickens and boils 1 minute. Stir a few tablespoonfuls into sour cream, then stir back into remaining in saucepan. Stir in catsup and dill weed; heat just to boiling.
4 Spoon meat balls into a chafing dish or heated serving bowl; pour hot sauce over.

Pacific Potluck

Bake at 350° for 25 minutes. Makes 8 servings

2 pounds ground beef

Three easy-on-the-hostess, economical meat ball casseroles sensational enough for parties (left to right): Scandinavian Ragout, served here with corn and crinkly potatoes, Saucy Dill Meat Balls and Pacific Potluck.

1 small onion, grated
2 eggs
2½ teaspoons salt
⅛ teaspoon pepper
2 tablespoons soy sauce
2 tablespoons vegetable oil
1 can (5 ounces) whole blanched almonds (1 cup)
1 can (about 14 ounces) pineapple chunks
1 can (1 pint, 2 ounces) pineapple juice
½ cup sugar
¼ cup cornstarch
½ cup cider vinegar
3 cups frozen peas (from a 1½-pound bag), cooked and drained
Hot cooked rice

1 Mix ground beef lightly with onion, eggs, 2 teaspoons of the salt, and pepper; shape into 32 balls; dip in soy sauce.
2 Brown, half at a time, in vegetable oil in a large frying pan; remove with a slotted spoon and place in a 10-cup baking dish. Stir almonds into drippings in pan; heat 1 to 2 minutes; sprinkle over meat balls.
3 Drain syrup from pineapple chunks and combine with pineapple juice. (There should be about 3 cups.) Mix sugar with cornstarch and remaining ½ teaspoon salt; stir in pineapple-juice mixture and vinegar. Cook in same frying pan, stirring constantly, until sauce thickens and boils 3 minutes.
4 Combine pineapple chunks and peas with meat balls and almonds in baking dish; pour sauce over; cover.
5 Bake in moderate oven (350°) 25 minutes to blend flavors.
6 Serve from baking dish with cooked rice or mound meat balls in center of a large shallow dish; spoon cooked rice around edge. Pass little bowls of diced bananas, chopped green onions, and East Indian chutney to spoon on top, if you wish.

Scandinavian Ragout
Dill and sour cream flavor this casserole combining meat, potatoes, cucumber and corn. Bake at 350° about 30 minutes. Makes 6 servings

1 pound ground beef
½ pound ground veal
1 cup soft bread crumbs (about 2 slices)
1 egg
1 small can evaporated milk (⅔ cup)
1 tablespoon grated onion
1 teaspoon grated lemon peel
1 teaspoon salt (for meat balls)
4 tablespoons vegetable shortening
6 medium-size (about 2 pounds) potatoes, pared and cut as for French-frying
1 medium-size cucumber, halved lengthwise and sliced ¼ inch thick
1 can (12 or 16 ounces) whole-kernel corn
1 tablespoon all-purpose flour
½ teaspoon salt (for gravy)
⅛ teaspoon pepper
1 cup (8-ounce carton) dairy sour cream
1 tablespoon dill weed

1 Mix beef, veal, bread crumbs, egg, evaporated milk, onion, lemon peel, and 1 teaspoon salt in large bowl; shape into 36 small balls. Brown on all sides in shortening in medium-size frying pan; place in mound in one third of buttered 12-cup baking dish.
2 Boil potato strips in salted water 5 minutes; transfer with slotted spoon to baking dish, piling in mound to fill second third of dish; save potato water for Step 4.
3 Boil cucumber slices in salted water 3 minutes; drain, adding liquid to potato water. Drain corn, adding liquid to potato-cucumber water, if needed, to make 1 cup. Toss corn with cucumbers; spoon into remaining space in baking dish.
4 Blend flour, ½ teaspoon salt, and pepper into fat in frying pan; slowly stir in the 1 cup of saved vegetable liquid. Cook, stirring constantly, until gravy thickens and boils 1 minute. Stir in sour cream and dill weed; heat just to boiling; pour over potatoes and meat; tip dish so gravy will flow evenly to bottom; cover.
5 Bake in moderate oven (350°) 30 minutes, or until bubbly-hot.

Continental Veal Casserole
So easy to make with canned chicken gravy. Bake at 375° for 1 hour and 45 minutes. Makes 12 servings

1½ pounds ground veal
¾ pound ground beef
1 cup coarse soft bread crumbs (2 slices)
2 eggs, beaten
1 teaspoon salt
½ teaspoon ground mace
¼ teaspoon pepper

2 cans (about 1 pound each) whole white onions, drained
2 cans (about 11 ounces each) chicken gravy
1 cup uncooked regular rice
1 package (10 ounces) frozen peas
1 cup (8-ounce carton) dairy sour cream
½ cup toasted slivered almonds

1 Mix veal, beef, bread crumbs, eggs, salt, mace, and pepper lightly with a fork in large bowl; shape into 48 small balls.
2 Layer meat balls and drained onions in a 16-cup casserole (or use 2 eight-cup ones); pour chicken gravy over; cover.
3 Bake in moderate oven (375°) 1 hour and 15 minutes, or until mixture is bubbling in center and meat is done.
4 While casserole bakes, cook rice, following label directions; drain; place frozen peas on top of rice in saucepan.
5 Measure out ½ cup peas for Step 7; stir remaining peas and sour cream into rice, then stir all into casserole.
6 Bake, uncovered, 30 minutes longer, or until bubbly-hot.
7 Cook the saved ½ cup peas in small amount boiling salted water in small saucepan just until tender; drain; sprinkle over bubbling casserole; top with a ring of toasted slivered almonds.

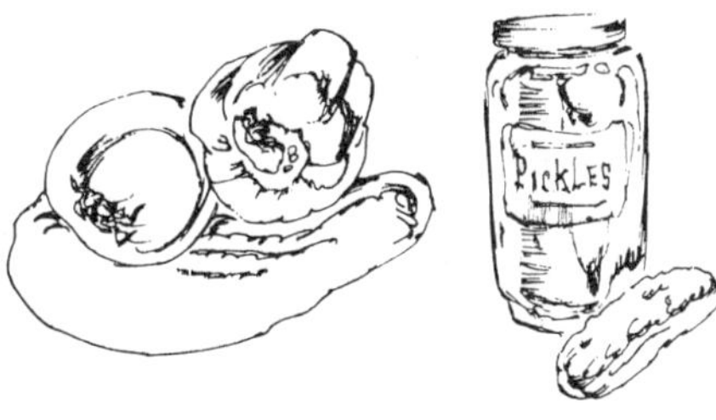

Lamb 'n' Curry
Makes 4 servings

1 pound ground lamb
1 small onion, grated
½ clove of garlic, minced
1 slice of slightly dry bread, crumbled
6 tablespoons milk
1 teaspoon salt (for meat)
1 tablespoon butter or margarine
1 medium-size onion, chopped (½ cup)
2 teaspoons curry powder
1 can (12 ounces) apple juice
1 teaspoon salt (for sauce)

1 Combine lamb, grated onion, garlic, bread crumbs, milk, and salt (for meat) in medium-size bowl; blend with 2-tine fork; form lightly into 16 medium-size balls.
2 Heat butter or margarine in large frying pan with tight-fitting cover; brown meat balls; remove from pan; save for Step 4; pour off fat; return 1 tablespoon to pan.
3 Sauté onion in same pan 5 minutes; stir in remaining ingredients; bring to boiling; simmer 10 minutes.
4 Add meat balls to sauce; cover; simmer 15 minutes, or until meat balls are cooked and flavors are blended.

Skillet Lamb Balls with Vegetables
Everything cooks appetizingly in the same pan, ready to go to the table
Makes 6 servings

1½ pounds ground lamb
1 egg
1 small onion, grated
½ cup fine dry bread crumbs
2 teaspoons cornstarch
1 teaspoon salt
½ teaspoon pepper
½ teaspoon ground ginger
¼ teaspoon ground nutmeg
1 cup evaporated milk
2 tablespoons vegetable shortening
1 can (10½ ounces) condensed onion soup
½ cup water
3 carrots, pared and cut in thin strips
1 package (9 ounces) frozen cut green beans
1 package (10 ounces) frozen peas

1 Mix meat, egg, onion, bread crumbs, cornstarch, salt, pepper, ginger, nutmeg, and evaporated milk in large bowl; form lightly into about 30 walnut-size balls.
2 Brown in melted vegetable shortening in large frying pan or electric skillet; pour onion soup and water over; cover; simmer 20 minutes.
3 Separate balls in pan to make room for piles of carrot sticks, frozen green beans, and frozen peas; cover; cook about 20 minutes longer, or just until vegetables are tender.

Cooksaver Tip:
Meat balls will be even size if you pat meat into a rectangle about an inch thick, then divide it: first in half, then quarters, eighths, and sixteenths, depending on what size ball you want.

Fruited Lamb Balls in Dill Gravy
Bake at 450° for 15 minutes, then at 350° for 1 hour. Makes 8 servings

Meat Balls

1 pound ground lamb
½ pound ground fresh pork

½ pound ground veal
1 large tart apple, pared, cored, and grated
1 large onion, grated
2 cups soft bread crumbs (4 slices)
3 eggs
¼ cup chopped parsley
2 teaspoons seasoned salt
1 teaspoon ground ginger

Gravy

2⅓ cups hot water
4 tablespoons (½ stick) butter or margarine
6 tablespoons flour
1 teaspoon salt
1 tall can (14½ ounces) evaporated milk
2 teaspoons dillweed

1 Make meat balls: Combine all ingredients in large bowl; mix lightly with a fork just until blended. Shape into 48 small balls; place, not touching each other, in a single layer in greased shallow baking pans.
2 Bake in very hot oven (450°) 15 minutes, or until lightly browned. Remove and mound in the middle of a shallow 8-cup baking dish.
3 Make gravy: Pour water into pans; stir to mix with drippings and baked-on meat juices. Pour into a 4-cup measure or small bowl.
4 Melt butter or margarine in medium-size saucepan; remove from heat. Blend in flour and salt; gradually stir in drippings mixture and evaporated milk.
5 Cook, stirring constantly, until gravy thickens and boils 1 minute; stir in dillweed. Pour around meat balls in baking dish; cover with lid or foil; chill. Remove from refrigerator and let stand at room temperature 30 minutes before baking.
6 Bake in moderate oven (350°) 1 hour, or until gravy is bubbly-hot. Garnish with a few sprigs of parsley just before serving, if you wish.

Calico Lamb Stew

Rosemary-seasoned meat balls and two vegetables simmer in a lemon-light gravy
Makes 6 servings

2 pounds ground lamb
1 cup coarse soft bread crumbs
1 small onion, chopped (¼ cup)
¼ cup milk
1 egg
2 teaspoons salt
½ teaspoon leaf rosemary, crumbled
2 tablespoons butter or margarine
2 tablespoons flour
2½ teaspoons grated lemon rind
¼ cup lemon juice
1¾ cups water
1 bag (about 2 pounds) frozen peas and carrots

1 Mix lamb, bread crumbs, onion, milk, egg, 1 teaspoon of the salt, and rosemary in a large bowl; shape into 1½-inch balls. Brown in butter or margarine in a large frying pan; remove. Pour off all drippings, then measure 2 tablespoonfuls and return to pan.
2 Blend in flour, lemon rind and juice, remaining 1 teaspoon salt, and water. Cook, stirring constantly, until gravy thickens.
3 Stir in vegetables and meat balls; cover. Simmer, stirring several times, 35 minutes, or until vegetables are tender.

Porkers

Makes 4 servings

½ pound ground pork
½ pound sausage meat
1 egg, slightly beaten
1 slice of slightly dry bread, crumbled
¼ cup milk
1 small onion, finely chopped
1 teaspoon salt
Dash of pepper
Flour
1 tablespoon butter or margarine
2 large onions, sliced and cut in half

1 Combine pork, sausage, egg, bread crumbs, milk, chopped onion, salt, and pepper in medium-size bowl; blend lightly with 2-tine fork.
2 Form mixture lightly into 16 medium-size balls; dust with flour.
3 Heat butter or margarine in large frying pan with tight-fitting cover; brown meat balls on all sides; remove from pan; save for Step 5.
4 Sauté sliced onions in same frying pan, stirring often, for 10 minutes, or until tender.
5 Add meat balls to onions in frying pan; cover pan; simmer 15 minutes, or until meat balls are cooked.

Continental Meat Ball Pie

Bake at 425° for 30 minutes. Makes 6 to 8 servings

1½ pounds meat-loaf mixture (ground beef, pork, and veal)
3 tablespoons flour
3 tablespoons vegetable oil
2 Italian hot sausages, sliced ½ inch thick
3 cups water
1 envelope spaghetti-sauce mix
1 can (6 ounces) tomato paste
12 small carrots, pared and cut in 1-inch-long pieces

6 *small zucchini, washed and sliced 1 inch thick*
1 *can (1 pound) whole white onions, drained*
1 *package piecrust mix*
1 *egg, slightly beaten*

1 Shape meat-loaf mixture into about 18 balls; roll in flour to coat evenly. Brown in vegetable oil in a large frying pan; push to one side; add sausages and brown lightly.
2 Stir water, spaghetti-sauce mix, and tomato paste into frying pan; cover. Simmer 15 minutes.
3 Cook carrots and zucchini together in boiling salted water 15 minutes, or just until tender; drain well.
4 Spoon meat ball mixture, carrots and zucchini, and drained onions into a shallow 12-cup baking dish.
5 Prepare piecrust mix, following label directions, or make pastry from your own favorite two-crust recipe. Roll out to a rectangle, 15x12; cut out 9 about-1-inch-wide strips.
6 Save 3 strips for rim of pie, then weave remaining over pie to make a crisscross top; trim ends. Cover rim with saved strips, pressing down lightly all around. Cut out tiny fancy shapes from remaining pastry with a truffle or small cooky cutter. (Bake any leftover pastry for nibbles.)
7 Brush pastry strips with beaten egg; place cutouts around rim; brush again.
8 Bake in hot oven (425°) 30 minutes, or until pastry is golden and filling bubbles up.

Country Kitchen Stew
Bake at 350° for 50 minutes. Makes 4 servings

1 *pound ground fresh pork*
1 *large apple, pared, cored, and finely chopped*
1 *egg, slightly beaten*
½ *cup finely crushed soda crackers*
1 *teaspoon poultry seasoning*
1 *teaspoon salt (for meat)*
Dash of pepper (for meat)
Flour
1 *tablespoon butter or margarine*

Speedy version of a slow-simmering French classic: Jiffy Cassoulet, based upon meat balls and beans and baked for only 1 hour.

1 can (1 pint, 2 ounces) tomato juice
1 medium-size stalk of celery, cut crosswise into thin pieces
1 medium-size carrot, pared and thinly sliced
1 small onion, thinly sliced
½ teaspoon salt (for gravy)
Dash of pepper (for gravy)

1 Combine pork, apple, egg, cracker crumbs, poultry seasoning, and salt and pepper (for meat) in medium-size bowl; blend lightly with 2-tine fork.
2 Form mixture lightly into 16 medium-size balls; dust lightly with flour.
3 Heat butter or margarine in large frying pan; brown meat balls on all sides; transfer to 2-quart casserole; pour any drippings from frying pan.
4 Combine tomato juice, celery, carrot, onion, and salt and pepper (for gravy) in same frying pan; bring to boiling; pour hot gravy over meat balls.
5 Bake, covered, in moderate oven (350°) 40 minutes; remove cover; bake 10 minutes longer, or until meat is thoroughly cooked, vegetables are tender, and gravy is slightly thickened.

Sweet-Sour Ham Balls
Makes 6 servings

3 cups ground cooked ham
½ cup fine dry bread crumbs
1 egg
¼ cup vegetable oil
1 can (about 14 ounces) pineapple chunks
3 tablespoons soy sauce
1 tablespoon brown sugar
2 tablespoons cornstarch
¼ cup cider vinegar
2 large green peppers, quartered, seeded, and cut in strips

1 Mix ham, bread crumbs, and egg in a large bowl; shape into 12 large balls. Brown in oil in a large frying pan; remove.
2 Drain syrup from pineapple into a 4-cup measure; add soy sauce, brown sugar, and water to make 2 cups. Stir into drippings in frying pan. Place ham balls in sauce; cover. Simmer 15 minutes.
3 Blend cornstarch and vinegar until smooth in a cup; stir into frying pan. Cook, stirring constantly, until sauce thickens and boils 3 minutes; stir in pineapple and peppers. Heat until bubbly. Serve over rice, if you wish.

CASSEROLES AND SKILLET DINNERS

Jiffy Cassoulet
Bake at 350° for 1 hour. Makes 8 servings

6 slices bacon
2 pounds meat-loaf mixture (ground beef and pork)
1 can (about 1 pound) red kidney beans, drained
1 can (about 1 pound) white kidney beans, drained
1 can (about 1 pound) sliced carrots, drained
1 can (about 1 pound) stewed tomatoes
1 tablespoon dried parsley flakes
2 teaspoons salt
1 teaspoon leaf thyme, crumbled
¼ teaspoon pepper

1 Sauté bacon just until fat starts to cook out in a large frying pan; remove and drain on paper toweling; set aside.
2 Shape meat-loaf mixture into a large patty in same pan; brown 5 minutes on each side. Pour off all drippings, then break meat up into chunks.
3 Stir in drained beans and carrots, tomatoes, and seasonings; heat to boiling. Spoon into a greased 10-cup baking dish; place bacon on top.
4 Bake in moderate oven (350°) 1 hour, or until bubbly hot and bacon is crisp.

Beef Crêpes Continental
Bake at 375° for 20 minutes. Makes 6 servings

Basic Crêpes (recipe follows)
5 tablespoons butter or margarine
3 tablespoons flour
1 teaspoon salt
¼ teaspoon pepper
2 cups milk
½ cup light cream or table cream
1 cup grated Parmesan cheese
1 medium-size onion, chopped (½ cup)
1½ pounds ground beef
1 can (3 or 4 ounces) chopped mushrooms

1 Make *Basic Crêpes* and bake; set aside while making sauce and filling.
2 Melt 4 tablespoons of the butter or margarine in a medium-size saucepan; blend in flour, ½ teaspoon of the salt, and ⅛ teaspoon of the pepper. Cook, stirring constantly, until bubbly. Stir in milk and cream; continue cooking and stirring until sauce thickens and boils 1 minute;

remove from heat. Stir in ¾ cup of the Parmesan cheese; keep warm.
3 Sauté onion in remaining 1 tablespoon butter or margarine until soft in a large frying pan; push to one side.
4 Shape ground beef into a large patty; place in same pan. Brown 5 minutes on each side, then break up into chunks. Stir in ½ cup of the cheese sauce, mushrooms and liquid, and remaining ½ teaspoon salt and ⅛ teaspoon pepper.
5 Spoon 2 tablespoonfuls of the meat filling onto each baked crêpe; roll up tightly, jelly-roll fashion. Place in a baking pan, 13x9x2; spoon remaining cheese sauce over top. Sprinkle with the remaining ¼ cup Parmesan cheese.
6 Bake in moderate oven (375°) 20 minutes, or until bubbly.

BASIC CRÊPES—Sift ¾ cup all-purpose flour and ½ teaspoon salt into a medium-size bowl. Beat 3 eggs with 1 cup milk and 1 tablespoon vegetable oil until blended in a small bowl; beat into flour mixture until smooth. Measure batter, a scant ¼ cup at a time, into a heated well-buttered 7-inch frying pan, tilting pan to cover bottom completely. Bake 1 to 2 minutes, or until tops are set and undersides are golden; turn. Bake 1 to 2 minutes longer, or until bottoms brown. Repeat with remaining batter to make 12 crêpes, buttering pan before each baking.

●

Beef and Onion Supreme

Bake at 375° for 1 hour. Makes 6 servings

3 medium-size Bermuda onions
1½ pounds ground chuck
1 large clove of garlic, crushed
1 package (10 ounces) frozen chopped spinach
1 teaspoon salt
1 teaspoon leaf rosemary, crumbled
¼ teaspoon pepper
1 envelope instant chicken broth or 1 teaspoon granulated chicken bouillon
1¼ cups water
1 cup light cream or table cream
1 cup soft white bread crumbs (2 slices)
2 tablespoons butter or margarine, melted

1 Cook unpeeled onions in boiling salted water 15 minutes; drain. Let stand until cool enough to handle, then peel and cut in half.
2 While onions cook, brown ground chuck in a large skillet; remove with a slotted spoon; reserve. Sauté garlic in same skillet; push to one side.
3 Add frozen spinach block; cook, breaking up spinach as it thaws until spinach liquid has completely evaporated. Return ground beef to skillet with salt, rosemary, pepper, chicken broth, and water; stir to blend well.
4 Arrange 6 onion halves in a 13x9x2-inch baking dish. Spoon meat mixture over; arrange remaining onion halves, cut side up, on meat. Pour cream over all; cover.
5 Bake in moderate oven (375°) 50 minutes. Toss bread crumbs and melted butter or margarine together in a small bowl. Sprinkle over onions. Bake, uncovered, 10 minutes longer, or until bread crumbs are golden.

Oven Beef Bounty

Bake at 350° for 1 hour. Makes 8 servings

1 package (8 ounces) elbow macaroni
2 pounds ground beef
1 tablespoon vegetable oil
2 cans (1 pound each) mixed vegetables
1 envelope onion soup mix
¼ cup sifted all-purpose flour
1 teaspoon salt
¼ teaspoon pepper

1 Cook macaroni, following label directions; drain. Place in a 12-cup baking dish.
2 Shape ground beef into a large patty; brown in vegetable oil in a large frying pan 5 minutes on each side, then break up into chunks. Remove with a slotted spoon and add to macaroni.
3 Drain liquid from vegetables into a 4-cup measure; add water to make 3 cups; stir in onion soup mix. Add vegetables to meat mixture.
4 Pour drippings from frying pan, then measure 4 tablespoonfuls and return to pan. (If needed, add enough butter or margarine to measure 4 tablespoons.) Stir in flour, salt, and pepper. Cook, stirring constantly, until bubbly. Stir in onion-soup mixture; continue cooking and stirring until mixture thickens and boils 1 minute. Fold into meat and vegetables; cover baking dish tightly.
5 Bake in moderate oven (350°) 1 hour, or until bubbly.

●

Meat Patties Cantonese Style

Makes 4 servings

1 pound ground round
1 egg, slightly beaten
¼ cup fine dry bread crumbs
2 teaspoons salt
Dash of pepper
¼ teaspoon ground ginger

¼ cup vegetable oil
½ pound green beans, tipped and cut into 1-inch pieces
1 medium-size red pepper, halved, seeded, and chopped
¼ cup chopped green onion
1 envelope instant chicken broth or 1 teaspoon granulated chicken bouillon
2½ cups water
3 tablespoons soy sauce
½ pound mushrooms, trimmed and sliced thin
1 can (5½ ounces) bamboo shoots, well drained
2 tablespoons cornstarch

1 Mix ground round lightly with egg, bread crumbs, 1 teaspoon of the salt, pepper, and ginger until well-blended; shape by rounded tablespoonfuls into 20 balls; flatten slightly to make patties.
2 Brown, half at a time, in 2 tablespoons of the oil in a large skillet about 3 minutes on each side; remove with a slotted spoon; reserve.
3 Add remaining oil; stir in beans, pepper, and onions. Cook, stirring constantly, over high heat 3 minutes. Combine chicken broth with 2 cups of the water; stir into vegetable mixture along with soy sauce and remaining 1 teaspoon salt; cover.
4 Cook over high heat, stirring several times, 10 minutes. Add beef patties, mushrooms, and bamboo shoots. Cover; cook 5 minutes longer.
5 Blend cornstarch with remaining ½ cup water until smooth in a cup; stir into meatball mixture. Cook, stirring constantly, until mixture thickens and bubbles 1 minute.
6 Serve with hot cooked rice, Chinese fried noodles, and additional soy sauce, if you wish.

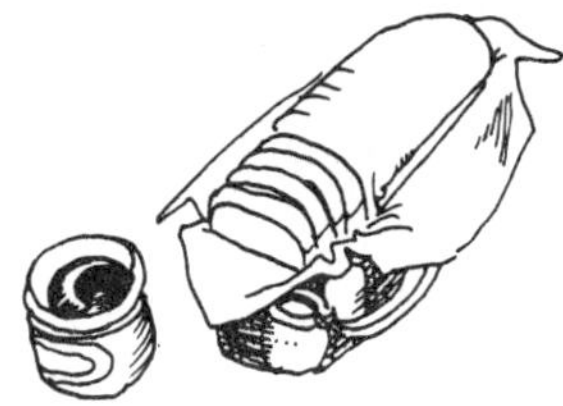

Cabbage-Burger Bake

An easy way to make popular cabbage rolls. Baking blends flavors perfectly
Bake at 400° for 1 hour. Makes 6 generous servings

1 small head of cabbage (about 2 pounds)
6 slices of bacon
1 medium-size onion, chopped (½ cup)
1 cup uncooked regular rice
1 pound ground beef
½ pound ground fresh pork
1 teaspoon salt
⅛ teaspoon pepper
1 can (about 15 ounces) spaghetti sauce with mushrooms
3 cups water

1 Quarter and shred cabbage. (You should have about 8 cups.) Spread half in buttered shallow 12-cup baking dish.
2 Sauté bacon just until fat starts to cook out in large frying pan; remove; drain and set aside for Step 5.
3 Stir onion and rice into bacon drippings in frying pan; cook, stirring constantly, over medium heat, until onion is soft and rice is lightly browned. Spoon over cabbage in baking dish.
4 Shape ground beef and pork into a large patty in same frying pan. Brown 5 minutes on each side, then break up into chunks. Cook, stirring often, a few minutes longer, or until no pink remains. Spoon over rice mixture in baking dish; sprinkle with salt and pepper; top with remaining cabbage.
5 Heat spaghetti sauce with water to boiling in same frying pan. Pour slowly over cabbage, so sauce will seep into layers underneath. Top with bacon slices; cover.
6 Bake in hot oven (400°) 50 minutes, or until rice and cabbage are tender. Uncover; bake 10 minutes longer to crisp bacon.

Jiffy Veal Tonnato

Makes 8 servings

2 pounds ground veal
1 cup grated pared raw carrots
1 cup dairy sour cream
1 small onion, chopped (¼ cup)
¼ cup fine dry bread crumbs
1½ teaspoons salt
¼ teaspoon leaf thyme, crumbled
Dash of pepper
2 tablespoons vegetable oil
1 can (about 4 ounces) tuna
½ cup dry white wine
1 tablespoon flour
1 envelope instant chicken broth
OR: 1 teaspoon granulated chicken bouillon

1 Combine ground veal, carrots, ½ cup of the sour cream, onion, bread crumbs, salt, thyme, and pepper in a large bowl; mix lightly until well-blended. Shape into 8 patties about ¾ inch thick.
2 Sauté in vegetable oil, turning once, until well-browned in a large frying pan.
3 Combine tuna, wine, flour, and chicken broth in an electric-blender container; cover. Beat until smooth. Pour over veal patties; cover.
4 Simmer, basting patties several times with sauce, 25 minutes, or until cooked through. Lift

patties from sauce and place on a heated deep serving platter.
5 Stir remaining ½ cup sour cream into sauce; heat slowly just until hot. Spoon over patties.

Burger Burgoo

Meat and rice simmer in a zippy tomato sauce to make this savory wintertime hearty
Makes 6 servings

2 pounds ground beef
1 large onion, chopped (1 cup)
1 cup diced celery
1 clove of garlic, minced
1 tablespoon sugar
1 tablespoon leaf basil, crumbled
2 teaspoons salt
⅛ teaspoon pepper
1 bay leaf
1 can (46 ounces) mixed vegetable juices
1 cup uncooked regular rice

1 Shape ground beef into large patty; brown in electric skillet, following manufacturer's directions for hamburgers, 5 minutes on each side, then break up into chunks. Push to one side.
2 Add onion, celery, and garlic; sauté 5 minutes, or until soft.
3 Stir in seasonings, vegetable juices, and rice; heat to boiling; cover.
4 Simmer 45 minutes, or until rice is tender and liquid is almost absorbed. Remove bay leaf before serving.

Beef Paprikash

Makes 8 servings

2 pounds ground beef
1 tablespoon vegetable oil
2 large onions, diced (2 cups)
2 cloves of garlic, sliced
2 tablespoons paprika
¼ cup sifted all-purpose flour
2 teaspoons salt
1 envelope instant chicken broth
OR: 1 teaspoon granulated chicken bouillon
1 cup water
1 package (8 ounces) fine noodles
1 cup dairy sour cream
¼ cup chopped parsley

1 Shape ground beef into a large patty. Brown in vegetable oil in a large frying pan 5 minutes on each side, then break up into chunks; push to one side.
2 Stir onions, garlic, and paprika into pan; sauté until onion is soft.
3 Sprinkle flour and salt over top, then stir in with chicken broth and water; cook, stirring constantly, until mixture thickens and boils 1 minute; cover. Simmer 15 minutes.
4 While meat simmers, cook noodles, following label directions; drain.
5 Stir about 1 cup of the hot meat mixture into sour cream in a small bowl, then stir back into remaining mixture in pan. Heat very slowly just until hot; stir in parsley.
6 Spoon noodles onto a heated deep serving platter; spoon meat mixture over top.

Chili Tacos

Makes 18 tacos

1 tablespoon vegetable oil
1 tablespoon chili powder
1 pound ground beef
1 can (1 pound) red kidney beans
¼ cup catsup
1 teaspoon salt
⅛ teaspoon pepper
1 can (11 ounces) Mexican tortillas
3 tablespoons butter or margarine
Taco Toppings (recipe follows)

1 Mix vegetable oil and chili powder in large frying pan; stir in ground beef and sauté, breaking meat up with a fork as it cooks, 5 minutes, or until beginning to brown.
2 Stir in kidney beans and liquid, catsup, salt, and pepper; cook slowly, stirring often, while fixing tortillas.
3 Carefully separate the thin pancake-like tortillas (there should be about 18). Sauté, a few at a time, in butter or margarine in a second large frying pan, 1 minute, or just until soft enough to roll. Or place tortillas on a large buttered cookie sheet; brush lightly with melted butter or margarine and heat quickly in a hot oven (400°) just until softened.
4 Spoon about ¼ cup hot chili mixture onto each tortilla; sprinkle with a TACO TOPPING; roll up. Wrap in a paper napkin and eat like a sandwich.

TACO TOPPINGS—Fill separate small bowls with finely chopped green peppers, cut-up green onions, chopped stuffed green olives, and grated sharp Cheddar cheese.

Jumble

Makes 6 servings

1 pound ground beef

1 tablespoon vegetable oil
1 medium-size onion, chopped (½ cup)
1 tablespoon chili powder
1 can (10¾ ounces) condensed tomato soup
1 cup water
2 cups uncooked wide noodles
1 package (10 ounces) frozen lima beans
1 teaspoon salt
1 cup grated Cheddar cheese (4 ounces)

1 Shape ground beef into a large patty. Brown in vegetable oil in a heavy kettle 5 minutes on each side, then break up into chunks; push to one side.
2 Stir onion and chili powder into kettle; sauté until onion is soft.
3 Stir in soup, water, noodles, lima beans, and salt. Heat, stirring constantly, to boiling; cover. Simmer 20 minutes, or until noodles and lima beans are tender. Stir in cheese until melted.

Hamburger Stroganoff

Brown beef and onion well, then heat in a mushroom sauce sparked with sour cream.
Makes 4 servings

1 large onion, chopped (1 cup)
1 tablespoon butter or margarine
1 pound ground beef
1 tablespoon all-purpose flour
1 can (6 ounces) sliced mushrooms
2 tablespoons chili sauce
1 teaspoon salt
1 cup (8-ounce carton) dairy sour cream

1 Sauté onion in butter or margarine until richly browned in a large frying pan; remove with slotted spoon and set aside for Step 3.
2 Shape ground beef into a large patty in same pan; brown over low heat about 10 minutes on each side, then break up into chunks; push to one side.
3 Blend flour into drippings in pan, then stir in meat, onion, mushrooms and liquid, chili sauce, and salt. Cook, stirring constantly and scraping browned bits from bottom of pan, until mixture thickens and boils 1 minute. Remove from heat.
4 Just before serving, stir about 1 cup of the hot meat mixture into sour cream in a small bowl, then stir back into remaining mixture in frying pan. Heat over *very low* heat just until hot. (Do not let it boil, for cream may curdle.) Serve over noodles or rice.

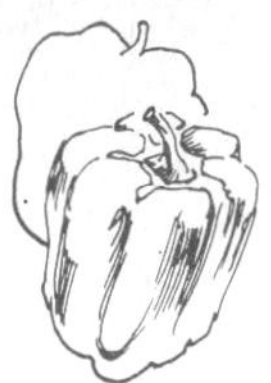

Stuffed Pepper Cups

Big garden peppers are heaped with a peppy meat-and-bean filling, then baked
Bake at 350° for 30 minutes. Makes 4 servings

4 large green peppers
1 pound ground beef
1 can (1 pound) pork and beans in tomato sauce
1 can (about 4 ounces) French-fried onion rings
½ cup catsup
1 teaspoon prepared mustard

1 Cut a thin slice from top of each pepper; scoop out seeds and membrane. Parboil peppers in a small amount of boiling salted water in a medium-size saucepan 10 minutes; drain well.
2 Shape ground beef into a large patty in a medium-size frying pan; brown 5 minutes on each side, then break up into small chunks.
3 Stir in pork and beans, half of the onions, catsup, and mustard. Spoon into pepper cups; place in a greased shallow baking pan.
4 Bake in moderate oven (350°) 20 minutes; place remaining onions on top, dividing evenly. Bake 10 minutes longer, or until onions are hot and crisp.

Enfrijoladas

Fill tortillas ahead, ready to arrange in their peppery tomato-and-bean sauce and add topping at the last minute
Makes 8 servings

Sauce

3 medium-size onions, chopped (1½ cups)
1 tablespoon chili powder
2 tablespoons olive oil or vegetable oil
2 cans (about 1 pound each) tomatoes
2 cans (1 pound each) pork and beans
1 can (16 ounces) tomato sauce
2 teaspoons sugar
1 teaspoon leaf oregano, crumbled
¼ teaspoon liquid red pepper seasoning
1 clove of garlic

Tortillas

1 pound ground beef
1 teaspoon chili powder
1 clove of garlic, minced
1 cup chopped green onions
½ cup sliced ripe olives
8 Mexican tortillas (from an 11-ounce can)
3 tablespoons butter or margarine
2 cups freshly grated Cheddar cheese (8 ounces)

Topping

1 cup dairy sour cream
½ cup chopped radishes

1 Make sauce: Sauté onions with chili powder in olive oil or vegetable oil just until onions are soft in large kettle; stir in remaining ingredients. (Stick garlic with a wooden pick so it will be easy to remove.)
2 Simmer, uncovered, 1½ hours, or until thick. Remove garlic.
3 Make tortillas: Mix ground beef, chili powder, and garlic in medium-size bowl; shape into large patty. Brown in medium-size frying pan 5 minutes on each side, then break up into chunks; remove from heat. Stir in green onions and olives, then 1 cup of the prepared sauce.
4 Sauté tortillas, two at a time, in butter or margarine in large frying pan, 1 minute, or just until soft enough to roll.
5 As each is heated, spread with ½ cup meat filling; sprinkle with 1 tablespoon grated cheese and roll up, then sprinkle top generously with cheese.
6 Place tortillas, seam side down, in a shallow baking dish or pan; keep hot in heated oven. (Or make ahead, then cover and chill. Reheat just before serving time.)
7 To serve, heat sauce to boiling; spoon into a large shallow serving dish. Arrange hot tortillas in two rows on top; spoon sour cream down middle, then sprinkle with radishes.

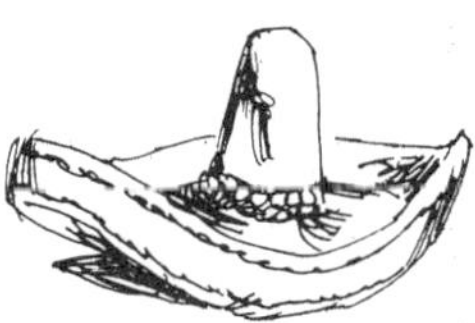

Empanadas

Bake at 400° for 18 minutes. Makes about 3 dozen small turnovers

½ pound ground beef
1 tablespoon vegetable oil
1 small onion, chopped (¼ cup)
1 teaspoon chili powder
1 can (about 1 pound) refried beans
1 teaspoon salt
1 can (about 2 ounces) deviled ham
1 hard-cooked egg, shelled and chopped
¼ cup chopped ripe olives
¼ cup chopped pimiento
2½ packages piecrust mix
1 egg
2 tablespoons light cream or table cream

1 Shape ground beef into a patty. Brown in vegetable oil in a large frying pan 5 minutes on each side, then break up into small chunks and push to one side.
2 Stir onion and chili powder into pan; sauté until onion is soft. Stir in beans and salt; simmer 3 minutes; remove from heat.
3 Stir in deviled ham, hard-cooked egg, olives, and pimiento.
4 Prepare piecrust mix, following label directions; divide into thirds.
5 Roll out, a third at a time, ⅛ inch thick, on a lightly floured pastry cloth or board; cut into rounds with a 4-inch cooky cutter. (Plastic top from a 1-pound coffee can also makes a size guide.) Place about 1 tablespoon of the meat filling on one half of each round; fold other half over filling; press edges together with a fork to seal. Cut several slits in top to let steam escape. Place, ½ inch apart, on large cooky sheets. Repeat rolling, filling, and sealing with remaining pastry and trimmings.
6 Beat egg slightly with cream in a cup; brush over turnovers.
7 Bake in hot oven (400°) 18 minutes, or until golden. Serve hot.

Hamburger Pizza

Bake at 450° for 20 minutes. Makes 8 servings

2½ pounds ground beef
½ cup soft bread crumbs (1 slice)
1 small onion, chopped (¼ cup)
2 teaspoons salt
¼ teaspoon pepper
½ cup milk
1 can (8 ounces) tomato sauce
½ teaspoon garlic powder
1 teaspoon leaf oregano, crumbled
1 package (8 ounces) mozzarella cheese, sliced thin
1 package (4 ounces) sliced pepperoni
1 can (3 or 4 ounces) sliced mushrooms, drained
2 cans (2 ounces each) rolled anchovy fillets, drained
2 pimientos, cut in thin strips
1 cup halved pitted ripe olives
2 cup grated Parmesan cheese

1 Combine ground beef, bread crumbs, onion, salt, pepper, and milk in a large bowl; mix lightly

Tamale Bake: a South-of-the-Border casserole made of ground beef, cornmeal, ripe olives, sweet green peppers and a chili-spiked, thick, rich tomato sauce.

until well-blended. Pat evenly over bottom and side of a 14-inch pizza pan.

2 Mix tomato sauce, garlic powder, and oregano in a small bowl; spread over meat; top with mozzarella cheese.

3 Arrange pepperoni, spoke fashion, in rows over cheese to divide into 8 sections; fill in sections with mushrooms, anchovies, pimientos, and halved olives. Sprinkle all with Parmesan cheese.

4 Bake in very hot oven (450°) 20 minutes, or until meat is done as you like it. Carefully spoon off any drippings. Garnish with sprigs of parsley, if you wish. Cut into wedges.

●

Tamale Bake

Bake at 400° for 1 hour. Makes 6 servings

1 cup yellow cornmeal
1 pound ground beef
1 medium-size onion, chopped (½ cup)
½ cup chopped green pepper
1 envelope spaghetti-sauce mix
1 tablespoon chili powder
1 can (about 1 pound) tomatoes
1 can (7 ounces) pitted ripe olives, halved
1 cup grated Cheddar cheese (¼ pound)

1 Cook cornmeal, following label directions for cornmeal mush. Pour about half into an 8-cup shallow baking dish; spread evenly. Pour remaining into a greased pan, 9x5x3; chill.

2 Press ground beef into a large patty in large frying pan; brown 5 minutes on each side; break up into chunks; push to one side.

3 Add onion and green pepper; sauté just until soft. Stir in spaghetti-sauce mix, chili powder, and tomatoes.

4 Heat to boiling, stirring constantly; remove from heat. Stir in olives and ¾ cup grated cheese. (Save remaining for Step 5.) Pour over cornmeal mush in baking dish. (This much can be done ahead; chill. Take from refrigerator 30 minutes before baking.)

5 Remove cornmeal mush from pan by turning upside down onto cutting board. Divide in half lengthwise, then cut each half into thirds; cut each piece diagonally to make 12 wedges. Arrange around edge of baking dish, sprinkle saved ¼ cup cheese on top.

6 Bake in hot oven (400°) 1 hour, or until bubbly-hot.

●

Taos Tacos

Bake at 325° for 30 minutes. Makes 6 servings

Filling

2 pounds ground lamb
1 envelope onion-soup mix
1 can (1 pint, 2 ounces) tomato juice

1 can (8 ounces) tomato sauce with mushrooms
¼ cup firmly packed brown sugar
2 tablespoons cider vinegar
2 tablespoons Worcestershire sauce
2 teaspoons salt
½ teaspoon leaf oregano, crumbled
¼ teaspoon leaf thyme, crumbled

Pancakes

3 eggs
1½ cups milk
1 cup sifted all-purpose flour
1 teaspoon salt
½ cup white or yellow cornmeal
2 tablespoons melted butter or margarine

Topping

2 cups (16-ounce carton) dairy sour cream
1 package (4 ounces) shredded sharp Cheddar cheese
1 medium-size green pepper, seeded and cut in thin rings
Cherry tomatoes

1 Make filling: Shape ground lamb into a large patty in a large frying pan; brown 5 minutes on each side, then break up into small chunks. Stir in remaining filling ingredients; cover.
2 Simmer, stirring often, 1 hour, or until thick.
3 Make pancakes: Beat eggs with milk; sift in flour and salt, then stir in cornmeal and melted butter or margarine; beat just until smooth.
4 Heat a 7-inch heavy frying pan over low heat; lightly grease with butter or margarine. Pour in batter, a scant ¼ cup at a time, tipping pan to cover bottom completely. Bake until pancake top appears dry and underside is golden; turn; brown other side. Repeat, lightly buttering pan before each baking, to make 12 pancakes.
5 Spoon about ¼ cup of the filling onto each pancake as it is baked; roll up and place, seam side down, in a double row in a buttered shallow baking dish, 13x9x2.
6 Keep pancake rolls warm in very slow oven (250°) until all are filled. (Pancakes may be filled ahead, then chilled until ready to bake.)
7 Make topping: Spoon sour cream in a ribbon between pancake rows; sprinkle with cheese; spoon any remaining filling beside sour cream.
8 Bake in slow oven (325°) 30 minutes, or until top is bubbly and pancakes are heated through. (If filled pancakes have been chilled, increase baking time to 45 minutes.) Garnish with green-pepper rings and cherry tomatoes.

Land-Ho Subs

Makes 8 servings

1 large onion, chopped (1 cup)
2 tablespoons vegetable oil
2 pounds ground beef
2 cans (8 ounces each) tomato sauce with mushrooms
2 teaspoons salt
2 teaspoons barbecue spice seasoning
2 loaves long thin French bread, split lengthwise and buttered
4 dill pickles, cut lengthwise in thin slices
4 tomatoes, sliced
4 slices (from an 8-ounce package) process Swiss cheese, each cut in 4 strips
16 green onions, trimmed

Two ground beef "greats": Land-Ho Subs, Taos Tacos

1 Sauté onion in vegetable oil just until soft in a kettle or Dutch oven; remove and set aside.
2 Shape ground beef into two large patties. Brown, one at a time, in drippings in same kettle 5 minutes on each side, then break up into chunks.
3 Return all meat and onion to kettle; stir in tomato sauce, salt, and barbecue spice seasoning. Simmer 15 minutes, or until thick.
4 Spoon mixture onto bread halves; top with pickle and tomato slices, then cheese strips.
5 Broil, 4 to 6 inches from heat, 3 minutes, or just until cheese bubbles up.
6 Stick 4 green onions, sail fashion, in top of each half; cut each long loaf in half for serving.

Veal Taormina

Italian food fans will go for this zesty combination of meat and eggplant in tomato-rich sauce
Bake at 350° for 40 minutes. Makes 6 to 8 servings

2 eggs
1 cup fine dry bread crumbs
1 large eggplant, pared and sliced ¼ inch thick
¾ cup vegetable oil
1 pound ground veal
3 cans (8 ounces each) tomato sauce
2 teaspoons sugar
1 teaspoon leaf oregano, crumbled
½ teaspoon leaf basil, crumbled
½ teaspoon salt
½ cup grated Parmesan cheese
1 package (8 ounces) sliced mozzarella or pizza cheese, cut into triangles

1 Beat eggs slightly in a pie plate; sprinkle bread crumbs in a second pie plate. Dip eggplant slices into egg, then into crumbs to coat well.
2 Brown, a few at a time, in part of the vegetable oil in a large frying pan, adding more oil as needed; drain slices on paper toweling. Wipe out frying pan.
3 Shape veal into a large patty in same frying pan; brown, adding more oil, if needed, 5 minutes on each side, then break up into chunks. Stir in tomato sauce, sugar, oregano, basil, and salt; simmer 10 minutes.
4 Layer one third each of the eggplant slices, meat sauce, Parmesan cheese, and mozzarella triangles into a greased baking dish, 13x9x2. Repeat to make 2 more layers of each, arranging the remaining mozzarella triangles in a pretty pattern on top.
5 Bake in moderate oven (350°) 40 minutes, or until bubbly-hot and cheese melts slightly. Garnish with ripe olive flowers, if you wish. To make, cut a slice from one end of each of 2 large pitted ripe olives for flower centers; slice remaining into thin strips. Arrange strips, petal fashion, around slices.
Hostess note—Casserole can be made ahead and chilled. When ready to bake, place in a cold oven; set heat control at moderate (350°). Bake 45 to 60 minutes, or until bubbly-hot.

Lasagna Pie

Bake at 350° for 30 minutes. Makes 8 servings

½ package lasagna noodles (from a 1-pound package)
1 pound ground round
1 small onion, chopped (¼ cup)
1 envelope lasagna sauce mix
1 can (1 pound) Italian tomatoes
1 can (8 ounces) tomato sauce with mushrooms
1 teaspoon sugar
½ cup water
1 pound ricotta cheese
2 packages (8 ounces each) mozzarella cheese, sliced
1 jar (3 ounces) grated Parmesan cheese
2 tablespoons chopped parsley

1 Cook lasagna noodles, following label directions; drain. Cool in a large bowl of cold water until ready to use.
2 Brown ground round in a large skillet; push to one side of pan. Sauté onion just until soft in same skillet. Drain off any excess fat.
3 Stir lasagna sauce mix, tomatoes, tomato sauce, sugar, and water into meat mixture in skillet. Heat to boiling; reduce heat; cover. Simmer 20 minutes.
4 Pour ½ cup of the prepared meat sauce into two 9-inch pie plates. Drain noodles; pat dry with paper toweling. Line the bottom of each plate with noodles, trimming noodles to fit the shape of the pie plate. Cover with a third of the ricotta cheese, meat sauce, mozzarella and Parmesan cheeses. Repeat to make 3 layers in both pie plates, ending with Parmesan cheese.
5 Bake in moderate oven (350°) 30 minutes, or until bubbly-hot. Let stand 10 minutes before serving. Garnish with parsley. Cut each pie into 4 wedges.

Our Favorite Lasagna

Bake at 350° for 30 minutes. Makes 8 servings

½ pound sweet Italian sausages

½ pound ground beef
1 medium-size onion, chopped (½ cup)
1 clove garlic, minced
1 can (about 2 pounds) Italian tomatoes
1 envelope spaghetti-sauce mix
1 pound lasagna noodles
1 tablespoon vegetable oil
2 eggs
2 cups (1 pound) cream-style cottage cheese
2 packages (8 ounces each) sliced mozzarella or pizza cheese
½ cup grated Parmesan cheese

1 Squeeze sausages from casings; mix meat lightly with ground beef. Shape into a large patty in a frying pan; brown 5 minutes on each side, then break up into chunks; push to one side.
2 Stir in onion and garlic; sauté just until soft. Stir in tomatoes and spaghetti-sauce mix; simmer, stirring several times, 30 minutes, or until slightly thickened.
3 While sauce cooks, slide lasagna noodles, one at a time so as not to break, into a kettle of boiling salted water. Add salad oil; cook, following label directions. (Oil keeps noodles from sticking.) Cook, stirring often, 15 minutes, or just until tender. Drain; cover with cold water.
4 Beat eggs slightly; blend in cottage cheese.
5 Line bottom of a lightly oiled baking dish, 13x9x2, with a single layer of drained noodles. (Lift each strip separately from water and hold over kettle to drain.) Cover with a third each of cottage-cheese mixture, meat sauce, and mozzarella or pizza and Parmesan cheeses. Repeat to make two more layers of each. (Our picture shows the top layer of mozzarella cheese arranged in crisscross and triangle designs.)
6 Bake in moderate oven (350°) 30 minutes, or until bubbly hot. Garnish with a ripe-olive "flower" and parsley, if you wish. (To make olive "flower," cut a pitted ripe olive lengthwise into sixths; arrange, petal fashion, around a whole ripe olive.)

Porkie Pie

Bake at 400° for 20 minutes. Makes 4 servings

4 medium-size sweet potatoes or yams
2 tablespoons butter or margarine
1¾ teaspoons salt
1½ teaspoons cinnamon-sugar
1 pound ground fresh pork
Dash of pepper
2 tablespoons flour
1½ cups water

1 Cook sweet potatoes or yams, covered, in boiling salted water in a large saucepan 30 minutes, or until tender; drain. Cool until easy to handle; peel.
2 Mash potatoes slightly in a large bowl, then beat in butter or margarine, ½ teaspoon of the salt, and cinnamon-sugar until smooth and fluffy.
3 While potatoes cook, mix ground pork with 1 teaspoon of the remaining salt and pepper. Shape into 16 two-inch patties.
4 Brown patties slowly, a few at a time, in a medium-size frying pan; place in a shallow 6-cup baking dish.
5 Pour all drippings from frying pan, then measure 2 tablespoonfuls and return to pan. (If needed, add enough butter or margarine to measure 2 tablespoons.) Blend in flour and remaining ¼ teaspoon salt; cook, stirring constantly, until bubbly. Stir in water; continue cooking and stirring until gravy thickens and boils 1 minute. Pour over meat in baking dish; spread mashed sweet potatoes over all.
6 Bake in hot oven (400°) 20 minutes, or until bubbly.

Ham-and-Swiss Sandwich Puff

Bake at 325° for 35 minutes. Makes 6 to 8 servings

2 cups ground cooked ham (about 1 pound)
2 cups grated Swiss cheese (½ pound)
½ cup mayonnaise or salad dressing
1 teaspoon prepared mustard
12 slices white bread, toasted
6 eggs
2¼ cups milk

1 Combine ham and cheese in a medium-size bowl. (Tip: Putting both through a food chopper, using coarse blade, speeds the job.) Blend in mayonnaise or salad dressing and mustard.
2 Spread on 6 of the toast slices; put together with remaining toast to make sandwiches. Cut each diagonally into quarters; stand, crust edge down, in a buttered baking dish, 3x9x2.
3 Beat eggs slightly with milk in a medium-size bowl; pour over sandwiches. Cover and chill at least 4 hours, or overnight.
4 Bake in slow oven (325°) 35 minutes, or just until custard sets. Garnish with parsley, if you wish. To serve, cut between sandwiches; lift onto serving plates with a wide spatula.

Our Favorite Lasagna, another great ground beef bake that rates. As shown here, it's topped with golden mozzarella geometrics.

A budget beauty the family will adore: bubbling Ham-and-Swiss Sandwich Puff.

BUYER'S MARKET

BUYERS MARKET: HOW TO MAKE YOUR FOOD DOLLAR BUY MORE, BUDGETSAVERS TO REMEMBER, SUPERMARKET ADS, 31 WAYS TO SAVE ON MEATS, SAVING WAYS WITH FRUITS AND VEGETABLES, HOW TO SAVE MONEY ALL AROUND THE STORE:

SOME GENERAL TIPS

Most of us wish we could trim the high cost of eating without actually lowering our standards. It's possible to accomplish both if we take the time to acquire a few good habits and a certain amount of know-how:

• **Make a habit of checking your newspapers regularly for weekly specials.** These generally appear in your local paper one day each week—on Wednesday in some areas, Thursday in others, possibly on still another day in your particular area. These specials offer valuable savings.

Since one-third to one-half of the average food bill is spent on meats, poultry and fish, meat specials are of obvious importance. Savings on meat alone can run as high as 25 percent of the total food budget.

Considerable savings are possible on fresh fruits and vegetables. Asparagus on special may cost 23¢ per pound while in comparable supermarkets the price is 59¢ a pound.

• **Keep your menus flexible to take advantage of unexpected buys.** It is certainly wise to plan a week's menus before you go marketing, so that you won't be tempted to buy what you don't actually need. Do, however, substitute the special buy for an item already on your list.

Turkey's always a money-saver so serve it year round.

Buy foods on the cost-per-ounce or fluid-ounce or per-pound basis. If your store has a unit-pricing system, that is to your benefit. If not, put your math to work. Carry a small pad and pencil with you if the division becomes a bit too much to do in your head. This small amount of effort can bring your bills down considerably. Also, do your own shopping, take plenty of time and know the prices of the items you buy.

Generally, the larger the can, the lower the price. Individual packaging can double, even triple, costs. (You must remember, of course, to consider comparative quality as well as price.)

As with all rules, there are exceptions; by checking, you'll spot them. For instance, two 7-ounce cans of tuna may cost a couple of pennies more, but would be a better buy than the larger can, which is only 13 ounces. Or, if your children love catsup and you usually buy the large size, it might be cheaper to buy several small bottles with a "2¢ off" label.

It's false economy to buy large sizes of perishable dairy products, or milk by the gallon—even though it's cheaper—unless you use these foods in about a week's time. Soft, unripened cheese, like cottage and cream, loses its flavor after about a week.

The President's Committee for Consumer Affairs states: "There is nothing more aggravating than opening the refrigerator door only to find food, just purchased, already spoiled. The open-dating of perishable foods by supermarkets is a valuable tool for the American housewife in combating this unnecessary waste." "Open-dating" is legislated locally, so you might not have it where you live.

• **Learn to read labels.** There are appreciable price differences between foods of identical quality in your supermarket. Compare ingredients in various packages. Experiment. Only after you have taken the time to compare ingredients, flavor and cost can you decide on the best buy in an informed way.

• **Figure your meat costs on the price per cooked serving rather than the price per pound.** To do this, simply divide the cost of the meat purchase by the number of cooked portions you'll get from the piece.

• **Buy foods in season.** Fruits and vegetables are usually lowest in price when they are at the peak of season. Frozen vegetables may be the best buy between seasons, but always compare them with canned.

• **Consider the quality you buy in relation to the way it is to be used.** If the food will be served at the table, where appearance and taste count, you may want a fancy quality; but in a recipe, where shape or subtle shading of flavor is lost in combination with other foods, a less fancy quality will do. For example, crisp shiny peppers would be important in a salad, as a garnish or for stuffing; but for frying slightly shrunken, cheaper peppers are better.

People will sometimes pay for perfection when it is really superfluous. Fruits with blemishes may cost you less, but are the same inside, and will do nicely for fruit compote or any other cooking or baking. Keep in mind, too, that you pay more for run-of-the-mill fruits and vegetables of medium size than for perfect larger ones.

Whole canned or frozen vegetables cost more than the cut style—simply because it is more difficult to keep them whole during the processing.

When someone cooks your dinner, chops your peppers, makes your pastry shell or even adds cinnamon to your sugar, you know that you must pay for these services. But do you always realize the additional costs for these conveniences—packaging, transportation and research?

By starting from scratch, you can cut your food costs by as much as 40 to 80 percent. Of course, you may still want the convenience of many of these products—and be willing to pay the price for the time saved.

If you have never baked a cake on your own, try something simple for a starter. A one-bowl cake method takes only a few minutes more of your time to sift and measure the dry ingredients than starting from a mix, to which you add water or milk, eggs and sometimes butter.

Consider cooking for two or more meals when you prepare a dish that requires long cooking, like stuffed cabbage, stew or even soups. You'll save on fuel, electricity and your precious time as well.

• **Snack foods are costly, so change your children's snack habits.** Offer them cottage cheese mixed with diced fruit, or a slice of American cheese with crackers, or fresh fruit. Your budget and their nutrition will benefit.

• **Buy day-old bread in the supermarket.** It's just as good as the bread you've kept in your bread box a couple of days. Besides, day-old bread is better for making sandwiches. If the weather is warm and humid, keep the bread in the refrigerator to prevent spoilage.

The French are famous for their cooking, as we all know, yet the French housewife is known for her *thriftiness* as well. Let it become that way with you. To reflect before tossing out food is a worthwhile habit to acquire: Those leftover string beans or stalks of broccoli are delicious marinated, then mixed with mayonnaise—particularly if you haven't overcooked or buttered the vegetables. The vegetables can be wrapped in aluminum foil and tucked into the lunch box along with a plastic fork. Or they can be added to the salad greens and tossed with a French dressing. After all, haven't you ever eaten marinated vegetables served as part of the hors d'oeuvres in a French restaurant, or as an antipasto in an Italian restaurant?

Those few pieces of boiled potato left from dinner can be quickly sliced and fried for breakfast with the scrambled eggs. Even the mashed potatoes can be made into patties or rolled inside a meat loaf, jelly-roll fashion.

The canned peaches you couldn't quite finish at supper can be used the next day as a hot-meat accompaniment. Simply drain them on paper towels and heat in their own syrup, with brown sugar to glaze. Or do them in the broiler, if you are broiling the meat.

Crusts cut from sandwiches can be used for stuffing or crumbs. Stale rolls can be used for crumbs, too: Toss in blender or grate them.

• **Learn how to substitute** less expensive meats, fruits and vegetables when prices rise because of shortages due to frost, strikes, etc.

• **Save on simple services.** Buy a large piece of meat and cut it yourself for stews, goulashes and meat pies. Do the same with poultry. Combine your own beans and franks; slice and grate your own cheese. The packaging and preslicing of luncheon meats and cold cuts almost *doubles* their price.

Besides reducing food costs, you will feel considerable pride in having managed your household effectively. Deservedly so.

BUDGETSAVERS TO REMEMBER ALL YEAR

Careful shopping pays off. Here's proof: If you save only five pennies on each meal, they will add up to more than $50 by the end of the year. That's a lot for just a little extra effort, isn't it? Reminders here—one for each day this month—will help you get the most from every food dollar

1 Get the midweek habit of shopping your newspaper's supermarket ad for all it's worth, for this is one of the greatest time- and money-savers. Find out what meats, fresh produce, frozen foods, and staples are on special, then work them into your weekend meals

2 Before you start out, plan your menus completely enough to guide you in making up a shopping list. Jot down items by departments to save steps and avoid forgetting anything. And remember to take your list with you

3 Take time to read labels and compare brands, grades, and sizes, for here are the keys to many savings. For example: Canned whole fruits make attractive salads, while cut varieties in baked desserts taste just as good

4 Learn to recognize a "feature special" and take advantage of it. This is a product on which your supermarket lowers the price to coax you into the store. If it's an item you use often, or it keeps well and you have storage space, it is a good food investment

5 Make oven heat do double or triple duty. Bake a stew along with a roast; or a big squash in the shell to peel, cut up, and glaze invitingly for another meal

6 Put a little fun in your shopping cart. Most families like surprises, and you'll enjoy trying something new. However, all "impulse" buying isn't good. It's better budgeting to pick up ideas from advertisements, then make a note on your shopping list to look for them

7 Consider ready-to-heat foods, for some cost less than those made at home. For example: A serving of canned vegetable soup figures out to about 5¢; fixed at home, a cent more

8 Remember that the price doesn't indicate how *good* a particular food is for you. Steak is steak and such pleasurable eating! But other cuts such as chuck or round provide the same boon to good health at a more economical price

9 Check sales of two, three, or five items for 00¢. They usually mean big savings if the foods are ones your family likes. Mix-and-match offers let you pick all of one kind or a combination of several

10 Cheese prices vary, with choices to suit all needs. Tips: Aged natural cheeses are the highest; the process varieties, particularly in large packages, are the thriftiest. All are rich in protein and good-for-you foods

11 Give puddings, sauces, gravies, and canned soups the creamy touch by adding evaporated or instant nonfat dry milk. Cup for cup, each supplies the same important nutrients as whole milk—at a big saving. And what perfect keepers!

12 Buy according to your storage space. Family-size bags of frozen foods are economical but do not hold well in the ice-cube compartment of a refrigerator

13 Bear in mind how much your family will eat. A small can is often the best choice for a twosome, for it gives mealtime variety and eliminates leftovers. To serve fresh fruits and vegetables at their peak in flavor, buy only for two or three days' meals at a time

14 Large cuts of meat on special mean a bargain in price per pound—as well as meat for several meals

15 If you shop only once a week, avoid waste by using up fresh produce and other perishables first. Rely on canned and frozen foods to carry you through meals the latter part of the week

16 Think of bacon as a flavor extra as well as a meat choice. A few slices, diced, cooked, and stirred into scrambled eggs, stretch a little a long way. The drippings make ideal seasoners for vegetables, salads

17 Fruits and vegetables that are reduced for quick sale rate consideration if you are buying for immediate use. Mellow ripe bananas to stir into bread, or apples to make into sauce, promise good eating and give you your money's worth

18 Compare the prices of meats and poultry with the number of servings you'll get from each pound. A rule of thumb: Figure on four servings from a pound of boneless meat, two servings from a pound with the bone in, and just one serving from a real bony choice

19 One of your biggest budget boosters—that's eggs. A serving of two can cost as little as 10¢—often even less—and it makes a perfect substitute for meat

20 In a budget squeeze? Depend on hearty, popular macaroni, noodles, and dried beans to see you through in the finest style

21 Budget-best chicken is in the bag! If you have a large family or a freezer, it pays to buy broiler-fryers packed two, three, or more in a plastic bag. The birds are cleaned and ready to roast, or cut up and turn into all kinds of family-good main-dish and salad treats

22 On your shopping list, jot down "alternates" in case one food is a better buy than another. A special on canned pears may mean savings over the fresh ones you wanted

23 Stretch the dollars you spend at the dairy case these ways: Buy chocolate milk for a treat; milk in half-gallon or gallon containers if your family uses a lot; large eggs for breakfast and small ones for cooking. (And pay no premium for white or brown shells)

24 No one ever seems to tire of potatoes, and thank heavens—for what would we do without this penny-wise vegetable? While it keeps well, buy only as many at one time as you can store properly. This means give them air in a cool dry spot away from direct light

25 Day-old baked foods—bread, rolls, cakes—are usually marked 'way down, but are as fresh as if you'd bought them yesterday and stored them at home

26 How pampered we American shoppers are, with our choice of 8,000 separate grocery items! Understandably, no supermarket has the space to stock that many, but we can always find a substitute. And being flexible is a good shopping practice

27 Please small fry with a treat from your supermarket's milk or ice-cream case. Flavors just grow and grow, and all—energy builders for them—are timesavers for you

28 Carry menu insurance—a stand-by meal for days when time flits by. Choices range from complete frozen dinners to canned and frozen main dishes and vegetables, ready to heat-and-serve

29 Tag ends of bread getting ahead of you? Save every smidgen to crush and use for a crumb topper for a casserole or a coating for

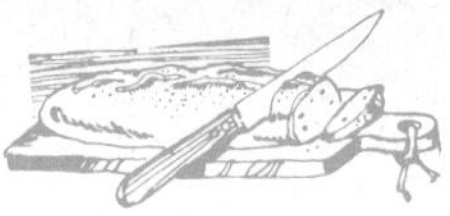

chops. Or cut in cubes and toast for croutons to float on soup or toss into green salads for crunch

30 You needn't always bypass items that seem to be a splurge, for they go a long way in dressing up an ordinary dinner. A frozen coffeecake that simply take heating or brown 'n' serve rolls, hot from your oven, make any meal lavish—and how they pamper a family!

31 Convenience foods or "instants" give you built-in maid service. And if saving time and work is important, they may be your best buys

IT PAYS TO READ YOUR SUPERMARKET'S ADS

The smartest homemaker in the world is the one who sits down with Thursday's newspaper and reads her supermarket ad for all it's worth. This is easy-chair shopping, and the time you spend will pay off in moneysaving *ad*-vantages. Easier on you and more fun in the end, you'll also have the satisfaction of knowing that you're getting the most from your food dollar. Let's see how it works

News in a nutshell

Each ad highlights specials on meats, good buys in seasonal fruits and vegetables, bargains in canned and frozen foods, pet-food items, and nonfoods such as cleaning and paper supplies. Actually, it's a news report from your supermarket buyers, who are always looking for good buys. These suggestions—printed right before you—help you to plan what you need before you start out.

Your first shopping step

When you are alone or the children are playing quietly, pour a cup of tea or coffee, take it to a comfortable spot, and go over your supermarket's newspaper ad. Have you ever really noticed how much good shopping information is crowded into so little space? (Sample ad that follows shows what we mean.) Look at all the specials and see how they fit into your family's food interests. In meats, do they like lamb, or will you surprise them with roast chicken? Both

FRESH MEATS

Tender Nutritious
BEEF LIVER Sliced or Piece lb. 00¢

U.S.D.A. Graded Choice Beef
7-BONE ROAST Pot-roast time is here lb. 00¢
LONDON BROIL Steak cut to broil quickly 00¢
BONELESS CHUCK For roast or stew lb. 00¢
Round Bone
SHOULDER STEAK For Swiss style lb. 00¢

GROCERIES

Chunk Tuna Ideal for sandwiches or fish loaf 5 6½-oz. cans $0.
Cling Peaches Yellow clings—choice of slices or halves 4 29-oz. cans $0.
Tomato Juice Pressed from whole ripe tomatoes. Healthful, vitamin-rich 4 46-oz. cans $0.
Sliced Pineapple Field-ripened 5 14½-oz. cans $0.
Early Garden Peas Taste-tempting and tender 5 16-oz. cans $0.

Unpeeled Apricot Halves 17-oz. can — Cream Style Golden Corn 17-oz. can — MIX 'EM
Stewed Tomatoes 16-oz. can — Whole Kernel Corn 17-oz. can — OR
Peas & Carrots 17-oz. can — Spring Pack Spinach 15-oz. can — MATCH 'EM
5 for $0.

U.S.D.A. Choice Shoulder
Lamb Chops lb. 00¢
Center cut (Blade or 7-Bone)

Round Bone Chops U.S.D.A. Choice Lamb Shoulder lb. 00¢
Lamb Rib Chops Serve broiled with pineapple slices. U.S.D.A. Choice Grade lb. 00¢
Breast of Lamb Excellent to stuff and bake lb. 00¢
Lamb Shanks Serve them braised or barbecued lb. 00¢

FRESH PRODUCE

Artichokes

Serve with melted butter or margarine
Extra Fancy
2 for 00¢

ASPARAGUS FANCY FRESH lb. 00¢
FRESH RHUBARB lb. 00¢
FRESH GREEN BEANS lb. 00¢

U.S. No. 1 Idaho Russet
Potatoes 10-lb. bag 00¢

NON FOODS

Paper Towels 2 00¢
Toilet Tissue 00¢
Aluminum Foil 00¢
Transparent Wrap 2 00¢
Waxed Paper 00¢
Paper Napkins 2 00¢

Detergent
Clothes White, Dishes Bright 49½-oz. pkg. 00¢

Liquid Bleach
Safe for nylon, rayon and dacron 00¢

FROZEN FOODS

French Fries Regular or Crinkle Cut 5 9-oz. pkgs. 00¢

NEW "POUR AND STORE" ECONOMY PACKAGE.
You pour out the amount needed and store balance in your freezer

Cut Green Beans 20-oz. bag 00¢
Peas and Carrots 2-lb. bag 00¢
Lima Beans 2-lb. bag 00¢
Cut Asparagus 2-lb. bag 00¢
Sweet Peas 2-lb. bag 00¢
Cut Golden Corn 2-lb. bag 00¢

DAIRY PRODUCTS

Fresh Creamery — Salt or Sweet
BUTTER 1-pound brick 00¢

Brown and White — Large Size
EGGS Fresh Gr. A 1-doz. ctn. 00¢

MARGARINE
1-lb. package 00¢ with your magazine coupon

FRESH MILK Homogenized 2 -quart container 00¢

BUTTERMILK BISCUITS
8-oz. can 3 for 00¢

ICE CREAM All Flavors ½ gal. 00¢

might be advertised good buys. Look at the fresh-produce, frozen-foods, and canned-foods columns, for they may suggest items you haven't served for some time.

Make a shopping list

Jot down the good buys—meats you will need for the coming week, maybe an extra cut on special to put away in the freezer. Add vegetable, fruit, salad, and dessert ideas for each meal. You'll see, without realizing it, perhaps, how your dinner plans are shaping up. And once the main meals fall into place, plans for lunches to pack, suppers, breakfasts, even snacktime treats come to mind.

Keep your list flexible

Here's where the "right to change your mind" really pays big dividends. At the supermarket you'll find unadvertised bargains too, and you may want to switch some of your choices. For example, fresh green beans may be especially attractive and low-priced, so buy them. Or you may have a hankering for fresh asparagus, but because it's just between the end of the growing season in one area and the start in another, the price is high. In this case, compare prices of both canned and frozen asparagus spears and cuts, for good buys are waiting here.

YOUR SUPERMARKET AD IS NEWS THAT MAKES CENTS

If you are up on your advertised specials, you can average a saving of 20% over nonspecials, and trim your food bills as much as 10%. Unbelievable? Proof of the pudding comes from a recent study made by the Food Research Institute of Stanford University. Says the report: Smart shoppers are those who look for these specials, make room at home to store them, keep menus flexible enough to use them, and, last, stay posted on the items that are featured oftenest. One reason a special may show up again and again is because it's in abundant supply. If it's a food the family likes, the shopper wins by stocking up.

If you are a new reader of supermarket ads:

- Lead off with the meat specials, for once they are chosen, the other foods will fall easily in place. If names like *7-Bone Roast** and *London Broil**, as in our sample ad above, are new to you, learn what the cuts look like. And notice the how-to-cook hints alongside each of these meats. When a big cut is offered, like fresh pork shoulder or chuck roast, think how you can turn it into dinners for two days. This is not only thrifty meal-planning, but you have a bonus of cooking only once for two meals.
- Take advantage of canned-food specials—three, four, and five for 00¢, and the mix-and-match combinations.
- Consider small can sizes if you are a twosome family, large ones for a big family, for no food is a bargain if it is wasted.
- Keep fresh-produce selections elastic. Look, compare quality and price with frozen and canned duplicates, then buy.
- Consider the big loose bag packs of ready-to-cook vegetables and fruits in the frozen-food cabinets. If you buy these, you can use just what you need and store the rest.

31 WAYS TO SAVE ON MEATS

Meat counters stock dozens of cuts that offer you the same good food value as well as economy. Follow these tips, and you'll be dollars ahead at the end of the month

1 Meat sales are one of the first steps to economy. The United States Department of Agriculture reports that the more expensive the cut, the less often it is featured. But when it does go on sale, the price drop is greater. For example, porterhouse steak may be advertised once in five weeks, but the price is then cut about 30¢ a pound. As a weekend special, even popular ground beef may be 10¢ a pound cheaper than usual.

2 Always buy well-trimmed meat with an even fat covering and lean flecked with fat—that's all you need for flavor. Remember that a roast at $1.29 a pound costs 8¢ an ounce, and any excess fat you trim away costs the same amount.

3 Which is thriftier—a thick family-size steak or thinner individual steaks for each serving? Surprising as it may seem, the family-size one. For example, a three-pound boneless sirloin cut 1¼ inches thick will make six servings. You'll need at least five pounds of T-bone steaks to serve six. At $1.59 a pound, the sirloin costs $4.77; at $1.49 a pound, the T-bones cost $7.45. The difference: $2.68.

4 For steak on a budget, choose chuck, bottom round, or shoulder steak. Marinate or ten-

derize the meat first, then broil or grill to medium-rare for maximum tenderness.

5 Chuck roast on sale? Buy a thick one; then, at home, cut it into pieces for a Swiss-steak dinner. Savings will be 20¢ to 30¢ a pound more than store-cut meat tagged *Swiss Steak**.

6 When porterhouse and T-bone steaks are the same price, pick porterhouse—it has a larger tenderloin.

7 Flank steak, sometimes marked *London Broil,* is not always an economical cut. One reason is supply; there are only two on each animal. For your money, the tender broiling steaks—porterhouse, T-bone, sirloin, or top round—offer more pleasurable eating.

8 Attractively priced alternates for a rib roast: Sirloin tip or rump roast. Prime or choice grades may be oven-roasted, are tops in flavor, and have little waste.

9 Beef-shank crosscuts, at least 1½ inches thick, make perfect individual pot roasts at penny-pinching prices.

10 For instant economy when your menu calls for beef Stroganoff, buy chuck or bottom round steak instead of the more expensive choices. Cut the lean meat into thin slices or strips and simmer until tender in bouillon or broth before adding the sour cream.

11 Most meat counters carry ready-cubed beef for stewing. But because store labor and meat trimmings cost money, you'll rate a double dividend if you buy beef chuck and cut it up yourself, then simmer the bone and trimmings for broth for soup.

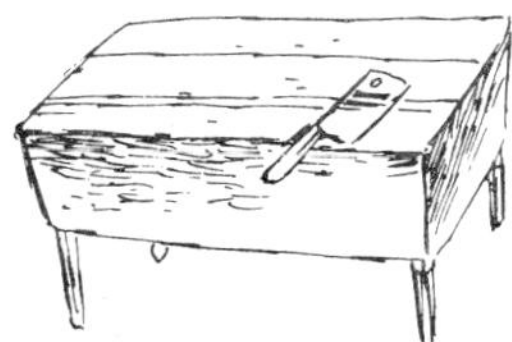

12 Watch for savings on large packages of ground beef. Those weighing more than five pounds often cost 3¢ to 5¢ a pound less than smaller sizes. If you have a freezer, make up several meat loaves and freeze part. Or shape a supply of patties and freeze for sandwiches or dinner meals.

13 Don't get hung up on ground beef. Ground lamb or veal patties are usually priced about the same as ground beef and give your menus a new lift.

14 When you want fresh pork, compare the price of pork shoulder with a leg cut (fresh ham). The shoulder may cost so much less that you can add on an extra pound or two of meat for the same total price.

15 Fresh pork hocks are a bargain when your budget's in a squeeze, even though it takes a pound for each serving.

16 Consider all ham prices and buy what fits your purse and purpose. Whole or half smoked hams are usually the same price per pound. And though a butt portion may be a few cents higher per pound than a shank end, it's a better choice because you get more meat. Center steaks or very thin breakfast slices are the most expensive.

17 Count on pork sausage for dinner as well as for breakfast—it makes an easy hearty meal. Your best buy: Bulk sausage. Because of fixing time and labor, patties are priced about 10¢ higher; links, about 20¢ higher.

18 Veal and lamb for stewing often cost less than the same cut of beef, and if your market is having a sale, you'll find these stew meats a delectable way to stretch your budget.

19 For keeping your budget and yourself fit, lamb breast really measures up.

20 All kidneys—beef, pork, lamb, and veal—are good buys with no waste. Prices remain fairly steady, and because all kinds work equally well in recipes, you can depend on what's available.

21 If tongue is a favorite at your house for platters or sandwiches, note that fresh tongue is more reasonable than the smoked variety.

22 Liver spells economy and good health. At the bottom of the price scale: Pork and lamb. Beef liver ranges from 10¢ to 20¢ higher, and the price of calf's liver is about the same as for steak. Braise or broil any variety, or grind for loaves.

23 Watch for specials on five-pound boxes of chicken legs or breasts. Compared to the same quantity in smaller packages, savings can add up to as much as $1.

24 On cost per serving, turkey comes out 'way ahead—and so will you if you remember that the bigger the bird, the more meat it will have in proportion to bone. As you shop, do a little arithmetic—half of a 20-pound bird may cost less than a whole 10-pound one.

25 Fancy-quality bacon may not be your most frugal buy. Use the regular sliced kinds for showy platters, but for sandwiches or recipe ingredients, ends and pieces, cuts, or slab bacon net big flavor at substantial savings.

26 Buy bologna in a chunk. If you slice it at home, you may cut as much as 10¢ a pound from the price.

27 Take a good look at canned meats—ham, beef roast, corned beef, chopped beef, luncheon loaves, meat in barbecue sauce, turkey, and chicken, to name just a few. Because every ounce is edible with no waste, the cost per serving is considerably less than for home-cooked counterparts.

28 Buy meat in terms of meals; leftovers that are not enough for a second time around are expensive.

29 Canned-meat meals are money- and time-savers, especially for small families. Corned-beef hash or roast-beef hash, chicken and dumplings, and spaghetti and meat balls vary from 17¢ to 23¢ a serving.

30 Use every bit of meat you buy. Melt down fat trimmings for drippings, and simmer bones and lean cuttings for soup stock or gravy. Time-saver tip: Shop for a week's supply of meat at once, trim it all before storing, then take care of the trimmings in one swoop.

31 In general, it isn't thrifty to buy on sales to stock your freezer. Why? Supermarkets routinely feature the same cuts, and there's no need need to tie up meat money in freezer inventory. A better plan: Buy extra cuts that appeal to you on any shopping trip and freeze them to use when needed. Veal, for example, isn't always available, but when it is, that's the time to buy enough for several meals and freeze it.

SAVING WAYS WITH FRESH FRUITS AND VEGETABLES

You can spend more time in the produce department of your supermarket than in any other spot as its gay colorful displays coax you to look and linger. Every day you'll find a variety of fresh fruits and berries, vegetables and salad greens to round out family meals, help you save money. Knowing what is a bargain and how to use it is your key to saving while spending. Here are tips to remember.

Be your own buyer

You are the best judge of what your family likes and how to cook it, so plan to shop yourself. Carry a list of items needed, but keep it flexible. Green beans may be your choice at home, but at the supermarket, fresh broccoli may look so tempting you can't resist it.

Take your time

Look around before you buy and see what is freshest, what family favorites there are. Splurge a little on asparagus, perhaps, then save a little on a carrot-and-celery dish. Keep in mind that your supermarket manager has bought the best the wholesale market has to offer for the day, so you have the advantage of his "pre-shopping" for you.

Consider more than price

Check the "why" of a special. Is it a seasonal food grown nearby? If so, your supermarket manager knows this and passes his bargain on to you. If it's a food your family likes, buy it. Specials on perishables such as bananas, pears, peaches, and melons that are ripe and ready to eat rate consideration. If you buy for serving right away, you have a bargain in good eating.

Keep in mind how much your family will eat

Most fruits and vegetables aren't the kind of items to stock up on, even with modern refrigeration. Buy enough for two or three days, but don't overload the refrigerator. It's too easy to tuck an item away and then forget it.

The biggest is not always the best

Large oranges and grapefruits, big potatoes and apples are not always your best buys. What counts is how you use them. For example, small citrus fruits, packed dozens in a bag, are perfect for juice, while the large thick-skin ones taste extra-luscious for eating out of hand. Small-size potatoes to boil and serve in their jackets save money, too. Little apples are just right for children because there's no waste; they're also good buys for making applesauce.

Through the eyes of a potato

When you put potatoes into your shopping cart, you're getting one of the best produce buys in your supermarket. Small new potatoes, big ones, thin-skin ones, and bakers are bagged and waiting for your choosing. And contrary to what you may think, potatoes are not fattening. It's how you serve them that may add calories. One medium-size baked potato is a treat even plain and figures just 90 calories. Top with a couple of tablespoons of cottage cheese and you add just 30 calories. One half cup diced plain boiled potato is just 50 calories; serve with

2 tablespoons medium cream sauce for 105 calories. If you fix the same amount as hashed browns, the calories jump to 235.

What are those green spots?
The skin on some potatoes may turn a slightly green color. It's nothing harmful; the artificial light in your supermarket is causing it. Since you want to see what you buy, your supermarket displays its potatoes in a transparent bag or one with a window. Exposed skins will show this greening. At home, store your potatoes in a cool dry place, away from direct light.

THE WHY'S OF PACKAGED PRODUCE

Imagine wearing your best white gloves and keeping them spotless while shopping for fresh fruits and vegetables! With each item graded, wrapped, and priced—perhaps even branded—ready for you to pick up, you can do just that. Supermarkets today try to display their produce the way their customers prefer it, so you'll find both prewrapped and pick-your-own, with shoppers lining up on both sides. Says the United States Department of Agriculture: *Young homemakers "love" prepackaged produce, but those who have been keeping house for years prefer to choose their own.*

It saves handling—The more any fresh produce is handled, the more likely it is to be bruised. To protect it, your supermarket may trim, wrap, and label each item right at the store, or it may be shipped already wrapped.

It is fresher—You will be able to buy some produce literally fresh-picked. Let's use lettuce as an example. As fast as it's harvested, it is trimmed of all outside leaves, wrapped in transparent wrap to protect its freshness, packed, and sent to market in a matter of hours.

It costs less to ship—Again with lettuce as an example: If packed in crates, the big outside leaves are left on to protect the heads, then they're trimmed at the supermarket. If trimmed at the fields instead, the saving in shipping costs is bound to be passed on to you.

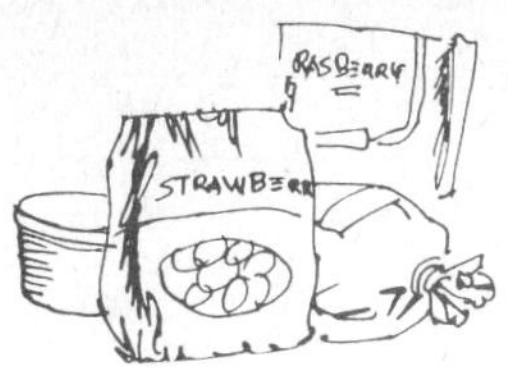

It is of standardized quality—Most of us depend on brand names for quality meats and canned, frozen, and packaged products. Why not produce? Some fresh fruits and vegetables are already available by brand name. More will appear as growers build packing plants close to harvesting fields and start their fresh produce off to market—fast.

Be patient. Prepackaged produce is the baby of streamlined supermarketing. As it grows, many of the reasons we think that we don't like it will be corrected, and we'll wonder why we didn't cheer it all along. Remember when packaged ready-cut meat was news?

HOW TO SAVE MONEY:

At the dairy case

Know the difference between Roquefort and blue cheeses and give each its rightful place in your menus. Both taste somewhat alike, but differ in price because Roquefort is made from sheep's milk and comes from France, while blue cheese is made from cow's milk and is produced widely in our own country.

Have children in your family? Treat them often to chocolate milk and chocolate drink, but be sure of what you're getting. The difference: Chocolate milk must be made with whole milk, while chocolate drink may be partly or all skim milk.

Give all dairy foods good care at home. This means keeping milk, butter or margarine, and cheese tightly covered or wrapped and chilled. Another reminder: To enjoy these products at peak flavor, buy often and only what you can use within a few days.

Make your egg money count—more! Compare sizes of eggs and prices and remember that size and color have nothing to do with quality. As a general rule of thumb, the United States Department of Agriculture gives this tip: If the price difference between sizes is more than 7¢ a dozen, you'll get more for your money by buying the smaller size.

Wonder why sharp Cheddar costs more than mild or medium-sharp? It all depends on age, for handling and storage cost money. Sharp Cheddar takes nine months or more for aging, while the time for mild and medium varies from one to nine months.

All around the store

In canned fruits, vegetables, juices, beverages, or soups, watch for advertised as well as in-store specials, and if they are choices your family likes and uses often, stock up. On the other hand, keep in mind that large sizes may not be bargains for small families if the leftovers are thrown out or spoil before they can be used.

Consider your time, budget, meal-fixing skill, the occasion, and storage space when it comes to ready-prepared, convenience, or instant foods. Some cost more and some less than cooking from scratch, and it's smart to take a few moments to figure out how costs stack up. Comparing the price of a cup of coffee made with the instant variety and one brewed from ground coffee is one of the quickest ways to prove to yourself how arithmetic pays.

Be an efficient shopper. How? Always start with a list as your guide, but be alert for hidden bargains. This means keeping a watchful eye out for unexpected "finds" while you're in the store. You may not have planned on buying apples, but if there's an attractive price on a 10-pound bag and your family likes apples, you'll stretch your budget by buying it. To save backtracking, make up your shopping list according to the layout of your market. If the produce counter is right inside the door, list those items first, then move on to the bread or meat sections, or whatever comes next.

Probably most important of all, no matter what you are buying, is to be an avid label reader, for here is your outside look at what's inside. Comparing weights, contents, and prices before deciding which product best suits your need is the secret to your greatest savings in food costs.

The biggest budget-stretchers, invariably, are foods in season. In America, the bounty is boundless.

INDEX TO RECIPES IN THIS VOLUME